First World War
and Army of Occupation
War Diary
France, Belgium and Germany

16 DIVISION
47 Infantry Brigade
Royal Munster Fusiliers
8th Battalion
17 December 1915 - 23 November 1916

WO95/1971/2

The Naval & Military Press Ltd
www.nmarchive.com
Published in association with The National Archives

Published by

The Naval & Military Press Ltd

Unit 10 Ridgewood Industrial Park,

Uckfield, East Sussex,

TN22 5QE England

Tel: +44 (0) 1825 749494

www.naval-military-press.com

www.nmarchive.com

This diary has been reprinted in facsimile from the original. Any imperfections are inevitably reproduced and the quality may fall short of modern type and cartographic standards.

© **Crown Copyright**
Images reproduced by permission of The National Archives, London, England, 2015.

Contents

Document type	Place/Title	Date From	Date To
Heading	WO95/1971/2		
Heading	16th Division 47th Infy Bde 6th Bn Roy. Munster Fus. Dec 1915-Nov 1916		
War Diary	Blackdown	17/12/1915	17/12/1915
War Diary	Farnboro So S.W. Stn.	17/12/1915	17/12/1915
War Diary	Southampton	17/12/1915	17/12/1915
War Diary	Havre	18/12/1915	18/12/1915
War Diary	St. Omer	19/12/1915	19/12/1915
War Diary	Fanquerie	19/12/1915	19/12/1915
War Diary	Verquin	20/12/1915	26/12/1915
War Diary	Vermelles	26/12/1915	26/12/1915
War Diary	Verquin	28/12/1915	30/12/1915
War Diary	Amettes	30/12/1915	31/12/1915
War Diary	Beavmetz Les Aires	31/12/1915	31/12/1915
Heading	8th Munster Fus. Vol. B2		
War Diary	Beavmetz Les Aires	03/01/1916	04/04/1916
War Diary	Lugy	05/01/1916	08/01/1916
War Diary	Beavmetz-Les-Aires	09/01/1916	15/01/1916
War Diary	Lapugnoy	15/01/1916	16/01/1916
War Diary	Houchin	16/01/1916	17/01/1916
War Diary	Lesbrebis	17/01/1916	24/01/1916
War Diary	Maroc	25/01/1916	31/01/1916
War Diary	Ames	09/02/1916	18/02/1916
War Diary	Bethune	19/02/1916	23/02/1916
War Diary	Norrent Fontes	26/02/1916	26/02/1916
War Diary	Bethune	27/02/1916	29/02/1916
Heading	8 Munsters Vol 3		
War Diary	Bethune	01/03/1916	02/03/1916
War Diary	St Hilare	03/03/1916	13/03/1916
War Diary	Haut. Rieux	14/03/1916	25/03/1916
War Diary	Philosophe	26/03/1916	31/03/1916
War Diary	Mazingarbe	01/04/1916	07/04/1916
War Diary	Front Line	08/04/1916	13/04/1916
War Diary	Front Line Hulluch-Left.	13/04/1916	13/04/1916
War Diary	Philosophe	14/04/1916	15/04/1916
War Diary	Batt In Support	16/04/1916	16/04/1916
War Diary	Tenth Avenue	17/04/1916	17/04/1916
War Diary	Batt. In Support	18/04/1916	20/04/1916
War Diary	Noeux-Les-Mines	21/04/1916	29/04/1916
War Diary	Left Half Puits 14 Bis Sector	30/04/1916	05/05/1916
War Diary	Left Half Puits 14 Bis	06/05/1916	08/05/1916
War Diary	Left Half Puits 14 Bis Sector	09/05/1916	10/05/1916
War Diary	Philosophe	11/05/1916	13/05/1916
War Diary	Philosophe East	14/05/1916	17/05/1916
War Diary	Mazingarbe (South)	18/05/1916	25/05/1916
War Diary	14 Bis Left Half	25/05/1916	29/05/1916
War Diary	Philosophe West G.13.d.a.5	30/05/1916	30/05/1916
War Diary	Philosophe West	30/05/1916	31/05/1916
Miscellaneous	Bombardment Of 28th May, 1916. 47th Inf Bde. No. 832/P.D.	28/05/1916	28/05/1916

War Diary	Philosophe	01/06/1916	01/06/1916
War Diary	Trenches Bde. Sup. Port Puits 14 Bis Section.	02/06/1916	07/06/1916
War Diary	Trenches Left Sub-Section Puits 14 Bis Section	08/06/1916	10/06/1916
War Diary	Noeux-Les-Mines	11/06/1916	16/06/1916
War Diary	Right Sub-Section Loos Section	17/06/1916	23/06/1916
War Diary	Bde. Sup. Port Loos Section	24/06/1916	28/06/1916
War Diary	Right Sub-Section Loos Section.	29/06/1916	30/06/1916
Miscellaneous	Extract from Brigade Routine Order dated 4.7.16, by Brigadier General E. Pereira. C.M.G. D.S.O., Cmdg. 47th Infantry Brigade.	04/07/1916	04/07/1916
Miscellaneous	A Form. Messages And Signals.		
Miscellaneous	Bloater		
Heading	War Diary 8th (S) Bn The Royal Munster Fusiliers 1st. July to 31st. July 1916		
War Diary	Right Sub. Section Loos Section.	01/07/1916	02/07/1916
War Diary	Bde. Support Loos Section.	03/07/1916	03/07/1916
War Diary	Mazingarbe	04/07/1916	10/07/1916
War Diary	Philosophe W Bde. Reserve	11/07/1916	13/07/1916
War Diary	Philosophe W. Bde. Reserve.	14/07/1916	14/07/1916
War Diary	Puits 14 Bis	15/07/1916	20/07/1916
War Diary	Philosophe W	21/07/1916	23/07/1916
War Diary	Philosophe	24/07/1916	26/07/1916
War Diary	Puits 14 Bis	26/07/1916	31/07/1916
Miscellaneous	8th (S) Bn. The Royal Munster Fusiliers. Appendix "A"		
Miscellaneous	Appendix B The 47th Inf. Bde. will carry out a Raid in the 14 BIS Sector to-night 29/30th July for the purpose of obtaining identifications.	29/07/1916	29/07/1916
Heading	War Diary 8th Royal Munster Fusiliers Vol 9 Month of August, 1916		
War Diary	Noeux Les Mines.	01/08/1916	09/08/1916
War Diary	Mazingarbe.	10/08/1916	12/08/1916
War Diary	Left Sub Section Loos.	13/08/1916	17/08/1916
War Diary	Bde. Support Loos	18/08/1916	21/08/1916
War Diary	Left Subsection Loos	21/08/1916	24/08/1916
War Diary	Les Brebis	25/08/1916	25/08/1916
War Diary	Marle-Les-Mines	26/08/1916	26/08/1916
War Diary	Burbure	27/08/1916	29/08/1916
War Diary	Sand Pit	30/08/1916	30/08/1916
War Diary	Citadel Camp-Guillemont	31/08/1916	31/08/1916
Heading	War Diary 8th Royal Munster Fusiliers Month of September 1916. Volume.		
War Diary	Barnafay Wood	01/09/1916	02/09/1916
War Diary	Guillemont	03/09/1916	04/09/1916
War Diary	Barnafay Wood	04/09/1916	04/09/1916
War Diary	Carnoy	05/09/1916	06/09/1916
War Diary	Ginchy	07/09/1916	09/09/1916
War Diary	Brickfields	10/09/1916	10/09/1916
War Diary	Vaux-S-Somme	11/09/1916	17/09/1916
War Diary	Huchenneville	18/09/1916	21/09/1916
War Diary	Meteren	22/09/1916	23/09/1916
War Diary	Locre.	24/09/1916	26/09/1916
War Diary	Bde. Support Line (Siege Farm)	27/09/1916	27/09/1916
War Diary	Bde. Support (Siege Farm)	28/09/1916	30/09/1916
Heading	War Diary Month of October, 1916. Volume 11 8th Royal Munster Fusiliers		
War Diary	Left Section 16th Divl Area (N.18.a-N.24.a)	01/10/1916	04/10/1916

War Diary	Bde Reserve Butterfly Farm (M.19.a.7.10)	05/10/1916	12/10/1916
War Diary	Bde. Support Siege Farm (N. 16.C.2.7.)	13/10/1916	17/10/1916
War Diary	Left Section 16th Divl Area (N.16.C.2.7)	17/10/1916	21/10/1916
War Diary	Divl. Reserve La Clytte (M.6.d)	22/10/1916	28/10/1916
War Diary	Bde Support Siege Farm (N.16.C.2.7.)	29/10/1916	31/10/1916
Heading	War Diary For Month Of November 1916. Volume 8th. R. Munster Fusiliers.		
War Diary	Support Battn Siege Farm (N.16.C.2.8.)	01/11/1916	02/11/1916
War Diary	Left Sector 16th Divisional Area	03/11/1916	06/11/1916
War Diary	Bde Reserve Butterfly Farm (N.19.A.6.9.)	07/11/1916	07/11/1916
War Diary			
War Diary	Bde Reserve	13/11/1916	13/11/1916
War Diary	Support Battn Siege Farm (N.76C.2.5)	14/11/1916	17/11/1916
War Diary	Northern Section ten Divnl Area	18/11/1916	21/11/1916
War Diary		22/11/1916	23/11/1916
War Diary		23/11/1916	23/11/1916

WORK/1971(2)

WORK/1971(2)

16TH DIVISION
47TH INFY BDE

8TH BN ROY. MUNSTER FUS.
DEC 1915 - NOV 1916

ABSORBED BY 1 BN NOV 1916

WAR DIARY
or
INTELLIGENCE SUMMARY

Army Form C. 2118.

8th Royal Munster Fusiliers
8.R.M.F.

Instructions regarding War Diaries and Intelligence Summaries are contained in F.S. Regs., Part II. and the Staff Manual respectively. Title pages will be prepared in manuscript.

(Erase heading not required.)

Place	Date	Hour	Summary of Events and Information	Remarks and references to Appendices
Blackdown	17/12/15	11.5 AM	Battalion 2 Coys. C & D march out for FARNBORO Station	
		12.40 PM	2 Coys. A & B " " "	
Farnboro' L.S.W. Rly.	17/12/15	1.55 PM	C & D Coys. entrained for SOUTHAMPTON.	
"	"	2.30 PM	A & B " entrained for SOUTHAMPTON.	
SOUTHAMPTON	17/12/15	4 P.M.	C & D " arrived	
SOUTHAMPTON	17/12/15	4.30 P.M.	A & B " arrived	
"	"	6 A.M.	Battalion & 100 Transport and Fatigue Party sailed for HAVRE on S.S. Empress Queen. C.O. in command	
"	"	9 P.M.	Transport & Fatigue Party sailed for HAVRE on S.S. Onward at 2 AM. Command O.C. 1/4 B.	
HAVRE	18/12/15	10 A.M.	S.S. Empress Queen arrived HAVRE	
"	18/12/15	7 A.M.	Battalion & 100 Transport & Fatigue Party landed & marched to HAVRE REST CAMP on arrival	
"			Mines fell 8 p.m. 18/12/15	
"	"	8 A.M.	S.S. Onward with Brigade Transport & Fatigue Party arrived. Baths arrived & came ashore.	
"	"		alone. Started to unload the ship about 11.30 and arriving June B. 11.30 and	
"	"	8 P.M.	Battn. marched from Rest C to Railway Station No. 5	
"	"		and the whole Battn. Transport entrained at 11.30 P.M.	
"	"		Ration strength at Rest Camp 2.38 officers and 928 men. One man admitted to Hospital	
ST. OMER	19/12/15	7.30 AM	Received orders to proceed to ANQUIERE	
FANQUERIE	"	10.30 PM	Battn. detrained & marched to VERQUIN & met C.O.	
VERQUIN	20/12/15	3 AM	All Coys. billeted 'A' Coy under Capt Cameron. B, C, & D Coys quartered in Barns etc	
"	21/12/15		Companies settled down & Cannon and Coy arrangement.	
"	24/12/15	11.45	Following officers N.C.O. & panelled returned to England to proceed to Kitchener in	
			application. Major Parsons 2nd in Command, Major R. Lake, Capt Peel (Adjt), Sgt Berkshire	
			Capt Hall 2nd Lieut. Hind, Infantry, Knox, Watson, Finnerty, C.S.M. Antony, C.S.M. Neal ... Sergt	
			Bateman 91 Ross (M Co), Sgt McQueen, S/Sgt Lewis (S) Burnell, Sgt Major S/Sgt Martin	
			O Sharp (S.I.) Cameron, Sale (F) O'Connor, Sgt R. Bolton. Sgt Frankton details

Army Form C. 2118.

WAR DIARY
or
INTELLIGENCE SUMMARY.
(Erase heading not required.)

PH Royal Irish Fusiliers

Place	Date	Hour	Summary of Events and Information	Remarks and references to Appendices.
VERQUIN	24/7/15	12 M.N.	It would not go owing to saboteur party. Capt. R. motor Ries 2 dispatch riders.	
"	24/7/15	4 pm	Fatigue party 400 strong under Capt. Baldwin and 15 officers paraded outside O Room prior to proceeding to the trenches at Cuinchy.	
"	"	10 m	2/Lt P. McMahon was wounded and conveyed to BETHUNE hospital	
"	26/7/15	12 45 am	2nd party of officers NCO's paraded outside O Room prior to proceeding to trenches, Capt Baldwin, Lieut Tarshis, Chandler, Beatty, Biggane & 2/Lt's Brennan S/W Fitzgibbon & S.M. Ginnty, CRMS Nash, CAMS King, CAMS Harmon, Sgts Fitzgibbon Howell, Buckley, Malone, Foley, Cyprus, Cole, Malone, Duncy & Tmooney relinquished command	
"	"	1am	Party commenced to trenches in Motor Bus	
VERMELLES	"	3 p	1st party NCO's & officers came from trenches & returned to VERQUIN by motor bus NOTAWALLET	
VERQUIN	28/7/15	6 am	Q.O.O. Cys. paraded outside O Room prior to proceeding to trenches via enjoying Tournehem on Hem	
"	29/7/15	7 am	Party returned. No Casualties	
"	"	12 noon	Lecture to officers by 2nd in command on points to be observed in the field & by the trenches. News received that 2/Lieut P.S. McMahon died of wounds received on 24/7/15) DAREBRETH & HARRIS at 8 am	
"	30/7/15	7 a.m	All Balln. out of billets proceeding to AMETTES.	
"	"	9.30	Balln. under C.O. marched to AMETTES via HESDIGNEUL, LABUISSIÈRE, MARLES-les-MINES, AUCHEL, CHAUCHYOLATOUR, FERFAY, BELLEAY, AMETTES	
AMETTES	"	4.40p	Balln. arrived at AMETTES & billeted for night.	
"	31/7/15	9.30 a	Balln. under E.O. left & proceeded to BEAUMETZ via HIRE via NEDON, NEDONSELLES FONTAINE-les-HERMANS, PALFART, MOOSART, LAIRES, BEAUMETZ-les-AIRES.	
BEAUMETZ-les-AIRES	31/7/15	1.30 p	Balln. arrived & billeted in BEAUMETZ, & at LIVOSART, BOR-PALFART.	

8th Munster Fus;
Vol: # 2

47/52

Army Form C. 2118.

WAR DIARY
or
INTELLIGENCE SUMMARY.
(Erase heading not required.)

Instructions regarding War Diaries and Intelligence Summaries are contained in F. S. Regs., Part II. and the Staff Manual respectively. Title pages will be prepared in manuscript.

5th Royal Irish Fusiliers

Place	Date	Hour	Summary of Events and Information	Remarks and references to Appendices
BEAUMETZ-LES- QUES	3/10	1.3 pm	"B" Coy. left LIBOART for BEAUMETZ-LES-AIRES. Arrived at 3 p.m.	
"	4/10	10.30 am	"B" " " " " " " 3.15 p.m.	
LUGY.	5/10	3.45 am	Batln. left. BEAUMETZ-LES-AIRES for LUGY.	
"	8/10	11.30 am	Batln. and Transport was inspected by Corps Commander Lieut Gen. Sir H.H. WILSON, K.C.B., D.S.O.	
BEAUMETZ LES-AIRES	9/10	8.30 am	Batln. & Transport moved to BEAUMETZ-LES-AIRES.	
"	11/10	9 am	Church parade & after Regtl. Inspection.	
"	12/10	10.30 am	Coys. commenced firing Musketry ammunition from the new Handbooks Reaufort Coys. firing on self inoculated range.	
"	13/10	8 am	Men practised Course of Musketry in the Line of Communication parades at 0 Room for Musketry Inspection.	
"	14/10	"	Boys firing all day	
"	15/10	"	do.	
"	16/10	"	do.	
LAPUGNOY	15/10	9 am	Batln. paraded under C.O. for LAPUGNOY. Without pack. Reconnaissance of French lines.	
"	16/10	3.30 pm	Move completed.	
HOUCHIN	16/10	10.30 am	Batln. under C.O. paraded for march to HOUCHIN. Pass carried on lorries.	
"	17/10	3 pm	Move completed.	
"	17/10	9 am	Batln. under C.O. moved to LES BREBIS. Full marching order. Cotton blankets carried on Transport.	
LES BREBIS	17/10	3.30 am	Move completed	
"	18/10	8 am	Boys paraded under Coy. Commanders for fatigue duties in R.E. trenches. Batln. handed over to R. E. for working parties.	

#353   Wt. W 3544/1454   700,000   5/15   D. D. & L.   A.D.S.S./Forms/C. 2118.

Army Form C. 2118.

WAR DIARY
or
INTELLIGENCE SUMMARY.

(Erase heading not required.)

2nd Royal Munster Fusiliers

Place	Date	Hour	Summary of Events and Information	Remarks and references to Appendices
LES BREBIS	26/9/15	10 a.m.	A party of B Coy. went working on our open road and killed one. 1223 Pte. McGRATH A. shot wounded, rifle other men.	5985 Pte Samuel T. 4318 " Power T. 5532 " Seymour J. 5876 " Purcell J. 1309 " Pettit F.
"		6 p.m.	Battn. paraded for MAROC. 2 Coys B & D for the 2.20 a.m. trenches at LOOS. A Coy for the trenches at MAROC. C Coy in 2d The Battn took over the trenches evacuated by the 2/K. LEINSTERS.	MAROC
MAROC	25/9/15	4 a.m.	Capt. O.G. de L. BALDWIN commanding B Coy. was killed by a shell. Reported & Jany. not known. 552 L/G. GIBBONS W. wounded.	
	26/9/15	1 a.m.	MAROC. Shelled heavily by hostile Artillery. No casualties.	
		5.30 a.m.	B Coy. marched out to LOOS to relieve C Coy. who took over D Coy's trench + 31 Pte. McCLARTY C Coy. wounded B Coy relieved A Coy. at MAROC. A Coy. taking over B Coy's trenches. 3820 Pte Brett M. admitted to Hospital Shell-shock	
	27/9/15	10 a.m.	4394 Pte. McGUIRE A. D Coy. wounded.	
	28/9/15	6 p.m.	A Coy. relieved D Coy at LOOS. C Coy. remained at MAROC. B Coy returned from the trenches at MAROC.	
	28/9/15		Casualties Nil.	
	29/9/15	5.30 a.m.	C Coy. paraded for trenches at MAROC.	

Army Form C. 2118.

1st Royal Munster Fusiliers

WAR DIARY
or
INTELLIGENCE SUMMARY.
(Erase heading not required.)

Place	Date	Hour	Summary of Events and Information	Remarks and references to Appendices
MAROC	29/10	5:30 pm	Casualties 1691 PTE BARRY 'A' Coy Wounded 1761 Sgt. O'TOOLE J. B " Shock 5937 PTE McSHERRY " " Poison 5788 " GUERIN T. D " Wounded 3658 " BARRY P " " 3613 " NOONE J " " 5713 " CRONIN S " " Now on duty. 3769 " HAYES M " " 5742 " MOFFAT T " " Now on duty.	
	30/10	6 pm	Capt. G.E. Bostock killed in action at LOOS at 3 p.m. Buried at MAZINGARBE. A stretcher bearer party from 'D' Coy went out in search of the party body. The gallantry of this party can only be appreciated when it is realized that the party had to walk across a road 2 miles long, that is shelled by the enemy & also within rifle fire range, and proceed to the scene of which they knew nothing, search for the body, return the same way. These men accomplished an almost task. They were 4890 L/C Hanrao T 'D' Coy 3835 " Pte. Blake P " 1601 " " McNamara T " 4521 " " Waught " 3621 " " O'Connor J " 4398 " " Walsh J " C286 " " Bullen A " 3890 " " Roberts T "	

Army Form C. 2118.

WAR DIARY
or
INTELLIGENCE SUMMARY.
(Erase heading not required.)

2/R Royal Munster Fusiliers

Place	Date	Hour	Summary of Events and Information	Remarks and references to Appendices
MAROC	30-7-16	6 p.m.	Casualties 4055 Pte Kenny P. Killed "A" Coy.	109.1770 LSgt. and 2 party P.L. men in
			4076 " McCann " Wounded "	6 M.R.O. Extract
			3708 " O'Connor " " "	4366 Pte Donohue
			4368 " Ford P. Killed " "	O'Connell " "
			3232 " Roomes " Wounded " "	4853 BREE.P.
			3221 " Woollard " " "	funeral
			1873 " Fitzgerald J " " "	3582 Pte Hennigan
			3310 L/C Ryan P " " "	4527 " Raymore
			1457 Pvt. Crotorty " Shot " "	3570 " Roberts
			8241 Pte. Herbert T. " " "	5739 " O'Connor
			4759 " Lane M " " "	
			2752 Cpl. Reynolds " " "	
			3820 Pte. Britt M. " " "	
			"B" Coy. relieved "A" Coy. at LOOS.	
	31/16	6 p.m.	Casualties "A" Coy. 6749 PTE O'Brien "A" Coy. Wounded	
			1513 L/C Ryder " " Wounded	
			5678 Pte. " " " "
			7 p.m. own artillery shafed the Huns for 1/2 an hour	
			6.15 p.m. "D" Coy. paraded to relieve "C" Coy. in the trenches at LOOS	

Certified True Copy.

M. Jinkinson
A.D.S.S./Forms/C. 2118.

Lieut. Col.,
Comdg. 2/Bn Royal Munster Fusiliers

Army Form C. 2118.

WAR DIARY
or
INTELLIGENCE SUMMARY.
(Erase heading not required.)

Place	Date	Hour	Summary of Events and Information	Remarks and references to Appendices
AME-S	9-2-16	7.30 AM	Programme of work for week ending 12-2-16	
			Tuesday Church Parade 7-30 to 8 9 to 9-30 AM 9.30 to 12.45 PM 2 to 4 PM	
			Inspection of rifles and feet Section Drill A) Range B) Bombing to Road March	
			Wednesday do do do	
			do B) Range C) Bombing D) Road march	
			Thursday do do do	
			do C) Bombing D) Route March A) Range	
			Friday do do do	
			do D) Route March A) Range B) Bombing	
			Saturday do do do	
			do A) Range D) Lecture to O Care of feet - billets Respirators	General clean up and Coy Arrangements

Army Form C. 2118.

WAR DIARY
or
INTELLIGENCE SUMMARY.
(Erase heading not required.)

Place	Date	Hour	Summary of Events and Information	Remarks and references to Appendices
AMES	10.2.16	9 PM	Extract from Battalion order. The following men have been selected for Mounting courses first in 1st Army Corps.	

A Coy
- 821 PTE ORISON
- 4006 " MURPHY
- 3806 " O'CONNELL
- 1706 " GOS
- 1640 " JORDAN

B Coy
- 2381 " SHAUGHNESSY
- 4142 " KERLEY
- 3515 " LYNCH

C Coy
- 3810 " SWEENEY
- 430 " MEHEA. M.

WAR DIARY
INTELLIGENCE SUMMARY.

Army Form C. 2118.

Place	Date	Hour	Summary of Events and Information	Remarks and references to Appendices
AMGS	11-2-16	9 AM	Helmert Battalion Orders	
			3858 Unpaid L/c BRADY B Coy L/c paid L/c vice	
			3288 L/c Smith (reverted) from 25-1-16	
			5417 Unpaid L/c to FLEMING B Coy L/c paid L/c vice	
			4444 L/c CURRY (reverted) from 5-2-16	
		9.30 AM	Gen. PARTIE R.A. inspected the billets area view the Battalion at work	
	12-2-16	9 AM	Received Battalion Orders	
			The undermentioned have been evacuated to England and are struck off the strength from those dates	
			3789 PTE GRACE. T A Coy 22-1-16	
			5979 " MOFFATT. W B Coy 27-1-16	
			5952 " O'RIELLY. W B Coy 27-1-16	
			4394 " MᶜGUIRE. W D Coy 2. 2. 16 per H.S. Sᵀ DENIS	
			4046 " WHITSELL H Coy 4-2-16 per H.S. COPENHAGEN	

Army Form C. 2118.

WAR DIARY
or
INTELLIGENCE SUMMARY.
(Erase heading not required.)

Instructions regarding War Diaries and Intelligence Summaries are contained in F. S. Regs., Part II. and the Staff Manual respectively. Title pages will be prepared in manuscript.

Place	Date	Hour	Summary of Events and Information	Remarks and references to Appendices
AMIENS	12-2-16	9 AM	Exhumed Bodies killed (Cont)	
			5958 PTE CARROLL M B Coy 6-2-16 Per H.S. CAMBRIA	
			5663 " DONOGHUE M C Coy 6-2-16	
			4318 " POWER J B Coy 6-2-16	
			1609 " RIELLY E B Coy 6-2-16	
		5 PM	Lieut HICKEY (Div. G.S.M. KNAPP) relieved as officer i/c 6 Connaught Rangers & 2nd Royal Munster Fusiliers at the cloisters in	
			Wormhoudt Houptines	
			Eweale Amacur	
			Flanolines Belle	
			abriches Oues Arctor Nthe 2nd Munster Fus Uphersen	

Army Form C. 2118.

WAR DIARY
or
INTELLIGENCE SUMMARY.
(Erase heading not required.)

Instructions regarding War Diaries and Intelligence Summaries are contained in F.S. Regs., Part II. and the Staff Manual respectively. Title pages will be prepared in manuscript.

Place	Date	Hour	Summary of Events and Information	Remarks and references to Appendices
AME S.	13-2-16	9 AM	Programme of work for 13th to 17th Feb 1916	
			Sunday. Church Parade at School at 10 AM	
			Monday. 7.30 to 8. 9 – 9.30. 9.30 to 12.45	
			a) Range	
			b) Squad Drill & B.F.	
			12 Noon Lecture by M.O.	
			c) Bombing Squad drill	
			PM.	
			2 – 4	
			a) Bombing / Squad drill	
			b) Range	
			c) Route march	
14-2-16			Tuesday.	
			a) Squad Drill & B.F.	
			b) Bombing	
			c) Range	
			a) Range	
			b) Route march	
			c) Bombing / Squad drill	
15-2-16			Physical Training	
16-2-16			Wednesday	
			a) Bombing – Squad Drill	
			b) Range	
			c) Squad Drill & B.F.	
			12 Noon Lecture by M.O.	
			a) Route march	
			b) Bombing	
			c) Range / Rapid loading	
			Inspection Gas Helmets Rifles &c	
17-2-16			Thursday	
			b) Musketry Drill	
			c) do	
			a. Clean up	
			b. do	
			c. do	

8353 Wt. W.3544/1454 700,000 5/15 D. D. & L. A.D.S.S./Forms/C. 2118.

Army Form C. 2118.

WAR DIARY
or
INTELLIGENCE SUMMARY.
(Erase heading not required.)

Instructions regarding War Diaries and Intelligence Summaries are contained in F.S. Regs., Part II. and the Staff Manual respectively. Title pages will be prepared in manuscript.

Place	Date	Hour	Summary of Events and Information	Remarks and references to Appendices
AMES	16-2-16	12 Noon	Inspection by 1st Corps Commander. Postponed on account of bad weather.	
			Ordered Battalion Orders 15-2-16	
			The C.O. has had pleasure to mark the following appointments:	
			1491 Corporal L/Cpl Buckley J. B Coy. to be Corporal B Coy. with effect from 13-2-16	
			Private B Coy. recorded with effect from 13-2-16	
			3249 Pte KENNEDY E. B Coy. to be corporal of C/pl with effect from this date.	
	18/2/16	11 AM	Batt marched to BETHUNE. attached to 33rd DIV	
			Arrived BETHUNE 4 PM	

Army Form C. 2118.

WAR DIARY
or
INTELLIGENCE SUMMARY.
(Erase heading not required.)

Place	Date	Hour	Summary of Events and Information	Remarks and references to Appendices
BETHUNE	14-2-16	2-3 PM	Batt marched to trenches by Companies to hold the line by companies for 3 days	
			A Coy attached to 18th R.F.Us at ANNEQUIN	
			B Coy attached to 16th K.R.R. at sector immediately N of LA BASSEE - BETHUNE Canal	
			C Coy attached to 20th FUSILIERS	
			D. Coy attached to 1st QUEENS at CUINCHY	
			Reports C Coy LIEUT OAKSHOT and Party went over the parapet on the night of the 21st and bombed a BOSCH sniper they were out about an hour	
			D Coy On the morning of the 20th 4870 PTE WHITE.D was wounded at 4-45 A.M.	
			On the night of the 20th the M.Guns claim one man (HUN) killed	
			3586 SGT. HUGHES shot a sniper	
			On the morning of the 22nd 3898 CASEY (M.G) were slightly wounded	

Army Form C. 2118.

WAR DIARY
or
INTELLIGENCE SUMMARY.

(Erase heading not required.)

Instructions regarding War Diaries and Intelligence Summaries are contained in F.S. Regs., Part II. and the Staff Manual respectively. Title pages will be prepared in manuscript.

Place	Date	Hour	Summary of Events and Information	Remarks and references to Appendices
BETHUNE	22/2/16	10 PM	Companies returned to billets	
	23/2/16	11 AM	Batt under L.O. marched to NORRENT FONTES arriving there at 5.30	
NORRENT FONTES	26/2/16	10 AM	Batt returned to BETHUNE	
BETHUNE	27/2/16	8.30 PM	Batt paraded to take over the line as a Battalion. Seeley I.O. 1st Batt Welsh acting as adjutant	
			A, B, C Coys in the firing line D Coy in reserve	
			The Batt held the line for 2 days.	
			Casualties A Coy — Nil	
			B Coy — Nil	
			C Coy 1795 Pte HICKEY D wounded 28/2/16	
			4752 " FENTON J killed 28/2/16	
			D Coy 5689 " CASEY M wounded 27/2/16	

Army Form C. 2118.

WAR DIARY
or
INTELLIGENCE SUMMARY.
(Erase heading not required.)

Instructions regarding War Diaries and Intelligence Summaries are contained in F. S. Regs., Part II. and the Staff Manual respectively. Title pages will be prepared in manuscript.

Place	Date	Hour	Summary of Events and Information	Remarks and references to Appendices
BETHUNE	29/2/16	10 P.M.	Batt'n arrived at BETHUNE and went into billets	

Forwarded
M.O.R. Wrangam Smith
Cmdg. 8th Royal Munster Fusiliers
1-3-1916.

8 Munsters
Vol 3

Army Form C. 2118.

8th Royal Munster Fusiliers
8 R M F

WAR DIARY
or
INTELLIGENCE SUMMARY.

(Erase heading not required.)

Place	Date	Hour	Summary of Events and Information	Remarks and references to Appendices
BETHUNE	1-3-16	11 AM	Battalion had the use of the Baths at College de Jeune Filles all day.	
	2-3-16	11 AM	Battalion marched to S? HILAIRE. Stragglers arrived at 4 P.M.	
S? HILAIRE	3.3.16	9 AM	Lecture to Officers by Brigadier on attacking trenches	
	4.3.16	9 AM	Company arrangements	
	5.3.16	9 AM	Church Parade	
		3.30 PM	Lecture to Officers (D Brigade) by Major General HICKEY on the attack. He also expressed his pleasure at the smartness of the Brigade	
	6.3.16	9 AM	Company arrangements	

Army Form C. 2118.

WAR DIARY
or
INTELLIGENCE SUMMARY.
(Erase heading not required.)

1/8 Royal Munster Fusiliers
8 R M 7

Instructions regarding War Diaries and Intelligence Summaries are contained in F.S. Regs., Part II. and the Staff Manual respectively. Title pages will be prepared in manuscript.

Place	Date	Hour	Summary of Events and Information	Remarks and references to Appendices
ST HILAIRE	7.3.16	4 PM	Batt under commanding Officer left ST HILAIRE for HAUT RIEUX and BAS RIEUX	
	8.3.16	7 PM	Company's escarques Billets ready at most of HAUT RIEUX	
	9.3.16	4 AM	Company arrangements	
	10.3.16	9 AM	Company arrangements Regards informes the Compound at work authographies reported for duty parties to 3 coy	
	11.3.16	9 AM	Company arrangements	
	12.3.16	9 AM	Church Parade	
	13.3.16	7 AM	Company parades attends at ABOUVENT	

Army Form C. 2118.

8th Royal Inniskilling Fusiliers
8 R. In. F

WAR DIARY
or
INTELLIGENCE SUMMARY.

(Erase heading not required.)

Instructions regarding War Diaries and Intelligence
Summaries are contained in F. S. Regs., Part II.
and the Staff Manual respectively. Title pages
will be prepared in manuscript.

Place	Date	Hour	Summary of Events and Information	Remarks and references to Appendices
HAUT RIEUX	14-3-16	9 AM	LIEUT J H B MILLS reported his arrival and posted to C Coy	
			C Coy paraded on musketry range from BURBURE & 4-5-10 on SW12	
			& boy range	
	15-3-16	9 AM	Coys paraded on musketry range from BURBURE to ALLOUAGNIE	
	16-3-16	9 AM	Coy arrangements	

Army Form C. 2118.

WAR DIARY
or
INTELLIGENCE SUMMARY.

(Erase heading not required.)

Instructions regarding War Diaries and Intelligence Summaries are contained in F. S. Regs., Part II. and the Staff Manual respectively. Title pages will be prepared in manuscript.

8 R 14 7

Place	Date	Hour	Summary of Events and Information	Remarks and references to Appendices
HAUT RIVER	17.3.16	9 AM	ST PATRICK'S DAY HOLIDAY. Church Parade at KILLERS.	
		12 Noon	BRIGADE SPORTS at ALLOUAGNE. 84 MUNSTERS won 5 events out of 7.	
			2Lt S. WATTS reported this unit for duty, posted to B Coy.	
			2Lt PROS reported this unit for duty, posted to D Coy.	
			MESSAGE Army Commander Genl MONRO. Please convey to all ranks my best wishes on St PATRICK'S DAY and my feeling of confidence that they will prove themselves to be worthy successors of their gallant IRISHMEN who always shewn themselves to be	
			Best of MEN. I wish from our hearts to you all the B.O.E. on St Patrick's Day.	

Army Form C. 2118.

8th Royal Munster Fusiliers
8 R M F

WAR DIARY
or
INTELLIGENCE SUMMARY.
(Erase heading not required.)

Instructions regarding War Diaries and Intelligence Summaries are contained in F. S. Regs., Part II. and the Staff Manual respectively. Title pages will be prepared in manuscript.

Place	Date	Hour	Summary of Events and Information	Remarks and references to Appendices
HAUT RIEUX	18.3.16	9 AM	Coy Arrangements	
	19.3.16	8 AM	R.C. Church parade at KILLERS	
		5 PM	Lecture BRIG GENL PARSONS on maps	
	20.3.16	9 AM	Coy Arrangements. Bombing, Range.	
	21.3.16	9 AM	Coy Arrangements Bombing, Range	
	22.3.16	9 AM	Coy Arrangements. Bombing Range	
	23.3.16	9 AM	Coy Arrangements Bombing Range 24/3/16 CAPT HEMWALL M.O taken off strength Lt J T Murphy came in his place	
	24.3.16	9 AM	Coy Arrangements Evening Ruth to march to Killers for entrainment to NOEUX LES	
	25.3.16	7 AM	Batt moves by R.R to train to march to PHILOSOPHE	
			MINES. Then marched to PHILOSOPHE	

#353 Wt. W3544/1454 700,000 5/15 D. D. & L. A.D.S.S./Forms/C. 2118.

…

WAR DIARY
or
INTELLIGENCE SUMMARY.
(Erase heading not required.)

Army Form C. 2118.

8th Royal Munster Fusiliers

S. R. M. F.

Place	Date	Hour	Summary of Events and Information	Remarks and references to Appendices
Philosophe	March 1916 26		Battalion in Brigade Reserve billets in "Corons de Mazingarbe" usually known as Philosophe. H.Q. in PHILOSOPHE.	8th R.M.F relieved 2nd Ox & Bucks M.I. Bat 2.
	28	4pm	Batt. became Brigade Support and D Coy moved up to Reserve Trench north of Loos and Maroc Puits 14 Bis. A Coy + B Coy (the remainder of the Btn being 2 & 4 of the 23rd 24th of each Coy) to TENTH AVENUE and M.G. Section to support 7. LEINSTERS opposite PUITS 14. BIS, C Coy remaining in PHILOSOPHE	
	29		Quiet. 1691 Pte BARRY. M. A Coy wounded.	
	30		A good many 5.9 inch shells dropped half a mile west of TENTH AVENUE and more in 65 METRE REDOUBT where 2 or 5 platoons were, but men were in deep dug-outs and not hurt Pte 4282 FEARON. J. Machine Gun Section D Coy. wounded " 4984 O SHEA. J. B Coy. wounded	
	31	9 a.m.	Machine Gun Section returned to MAZINGARBE Some more shells on 65 METRE REDOUBT. A stray shell near VICTORIA STATION caused the following casualties 4054 SCARRY. C B Coy Wounded slightly Mess Cpl 3532 DOHERTY. F D Coy Wounded slightly Pte	
		5pm	Brigade went to reserve and Battalion to MAZINGARBE	M.O'Williams Lieut Col. 8th Royal Munster Fusiliers

31/3/16

WAR DIARY

INTELLIGENCE SUMMARY

Place	Date	Hour	Summary of Events and Information	Remarks and references to Appendices
MAZINGARBE	April 1/16		Battalion bathing and finding numerous working parties	
	2		More working parties in trenches. The following appeared in Batt. Orders "My Corps Commander (I Corps) wishes to express his appreciation of the following act of courage on the part of No 1453 Cpl TIMONEY J 8th RMF	
			On the 1st March 1916 a class of men was under instruction in throwing live Mills grenades from the West Spring Gun when a grenade the fuze of which was burning accidentally fell from the gun. No 1453 Cpl TIMONEY J 8th RMF picked up the grenade & calling to the men to get down threw it almost 30 yards when it exploded in the air. Had this NCO not acted with such promptitude, no doubt some loss of life would have occurred as the men of the class were standing from 4 to 5 yards behind the gun. The direct result of this NCO's gallantry and presence of mind was that only one man was slightly wounded in the arm. The Corps Commander wishes it to be known that had	

Army Form C. 2118.

WAR DIARY
or
INTELLIGENCE SUMMARY.
(Erase heading not required.)

Instructions regarding War Diaries and Intelligence Summaries are contained in F. S. Regs., Part II. and the Staff Manual respectively. Title pages will be prepared in manuscript.

Place	Date	Hour	Summary of Events and Information	Remarks and references to Appendices
MAZINGARBE	2 April 1916		This act of gallantry taken place in the firing line instead of at a class of instruction Cpl TIMONEY would have been eligible for recommendation for a higher honour. A record of the above will be made in the regimental conduct sheet of this N.C.C. in accordance with paragraph 1919 (xiv) King's Regs.,"	
	3		Weather fine & hot	
	4		Weather fine & hot. 1 man wounded. Weather cooler. C.O. and O.C. Companies reconnoitred positions between CORONS du RUTOIRE and MAZINGARBE to be occupied in case of attack	
	5		Advance party went to front line trenches in left half of HULLUCH sector to take over from 9th R.M.F. Battalion took over their trenches at about 6 p.m. They were dry and clean but in the centre very narrow and uncomfortable. A Coy on the right, B in centre, C on left and D in RESERVE TRENCH, as several mines had already been blown & more were expected opposite B Coy. This	
	6			

WAR DIARY
or
INTELLIGENCE SUMMARY.

Place	Date	Hour	Summary of Events and Information	Remarks and references to Appendices
	6/4/16		part of fire trench was lightly held. Warfare was primarily carried on during our stay in these trenches by Rifle Grenades aerial torpedoes enemy shelled us lightly & ineffectively every day with shrapnel. C Coy could not use rifle grenades until the NEWTON PIPPINS were sent up as the German line was 200 yds away. These latter were a great success in annoying the Germans and they replied with whiz-bangs.	
	7th		A wet morning made the trenches which are all in chalk greasy. Our trench mortars (light & 33 lbs)	
		2.30 pm	had a rather successful strafe.	
		7.30 pm	A mine went up a mile to the north end of the salient rapid & M.G fire spread to us. We and the enemy fired hotly for half an hour. There were no casualties among our men lining the parapet. There was no shelling. The R.E wanted to put up a mine of our own so the we stood to from 9 p.m till midnight when they fired it. A M.G fired into the following morning.	

Army Form C. 2118.

WAR DIARY
or
INTELLIGENCE SUMMARY.
(Erase heading not required.)

Instructions regarding War Diaries and Intelligence
Summaries are contained in F. S. Regs., Part II.
and the Staff Manual respectively. Title pages
will be prepared in manuscript.

Place	Date	Hour	Summary of Events and Information	Remarks and references to Appendices
Front Line	1916 7 April		Casualties 1 man A Coy wounded 1 Sgt + 1 man E Coy wounded; Sergt Twomey 1453 wounded on patrol. he died next of ep.	
	8th	6 a.m.	We blew a little mine (known as ROCHE'S crater). Lt McCLARTY and the bombers occupied it temporarily without resistance. We opened rapid fire on enemy's parapet but he did not show up, and in a few minutes everything was quiet. Enemy were very free with Rifle grenades all day and the following night much more so than foregoing day and then were several signs that a relief had taken place. a German was seen with a red band round a grey cap. Casualties 1 sergeant + 3 men wounded.	
	9		There was a free exchange of rifle grenades, aerial torpedoes (small) and T M bombs and our supports & reserve lines were shelled with shrapnel + H E Casualties 2 men killed + 3 men wounded	
	10		About the same as yesterday. Gen PEREIRA came round trenches. Casualties Lt A.N. OAKSHOTT wounded 1 man killed 4 men wounded.	

Lt A.N. OAKSHOTT

*353 Wt W2544/1454 700,000 5/15 D.D.&L. A.D.S.S./Forms/C. 2118.

WAR DIARY
or
INTELLIGENCE SUMMARY.
(Erase heading not required.)

Army Form C. 2118.

Place	Date	Hour	Summary of Events and Information	Remarks and references to Appendices
	1916 April 11	8.30am	Enemy blew a small mine between TRALEE & SMITH'S craters which did no damage either above or below ground. He did not occupy it. The Germans now apparently no have black & white exp bomb and it seems as if they had been relieved again. Casualties 2 men wounded. I died next day	
		2am	After the mine had set two patrols went out to reconnoitre MUNSTER TRALEE & SMITHS craters. The second patrol under Lt MCCLARTY was fired on at about 20 yds range by a party working on a sap, but managed to return safely. B & C Coys did some wiring on their front at the same time	
		6pm	A Lewis gun of ours firing from TRALEE CRATER killed 2 out of a party of 9 Germans working at their parapet.	MW 1093

Army Form C. 2118.

WAR DIARY
or
INTELLIGENCE SUMMARY.
(Erase heading not required.)

Instructions regarding War Diaries and Intelligence Summaries are contained in F. S. Regs., Part II. and the Staff Manual respectively. Title pages will be prepared in manuscript.

Place	Date	Hour	Summary of Events and Information	Remarks and references to Appendices
FRONT LINE	April 1916 12th	9.40 a.m. & 4 p.m.	There were exchanges of rifle grenades in which we had the advantage. Enemy retaliated with stg-bangs. Our artillery support slow and not very efficient owing to the fact that 50% at least of our whiz-bangs were duds. A STOKES gun on the other hand, which had not been brought up, fired 10 rounds, 8 of which were believed to have burst in the enemy's fire-trench.	
		7 p.m. to midnight.	Some exchange of rifle grenades. Casualties 5 men wounded.	
	13th		A quiet day. We were relieved during the day by the 7th LEINSTER REGT. We left the trenches much better than we found them, having provided head-cover against grenades + shrapnel at many traverses as well as putting out about 60 yds of post wire + wire balls between CARDIFF SAP & MUNSTER CRATER.	

Place	Date	Hour	Summary of Events and Information	Remarks and references to Appendices
FRONT LINE HULLUCH – Left	Ap. 1916 13th		During our stay working parties from 8th ROYAL IRISH & 7th LEINSTERS had been removing excavated material from the mine shaft and the latter had dug a new communication trench between front & support lines 50yds S of HAY ALLEY. Our stretcher-bearers had a very arduous time as some of the trenches were extremely narrow and it was difficult to get a man along and impossible to bring a stretcher.	
		afternoon	Batt arrived at PHILOSOPHE where it billeted by the Cross Roads. Weather fine Casualties 1 man killed 2 men wounded	
PHILOSOPHE X	14th		Batt in Reserve Casualties 1 man wounded The following is a Minute from the Brigadier on 13th inst "The very thorough & satisfactory system of patrolling adopted by	

Army Form C. 2118.

WAR DIARY
or
INTELLIGENCE SUMMARY.

(Erase heading not required.)

Instructions regarding War Diaries and Intelligence Summaries are contained in F. S. Regs., Part II. and the Staff Manual respectively. Title pages will be prepared in manuscript.

Place	Date	Hour	Summary of Events and Information	Remarks and references to Appendices
	April 1916		"you last night together with Major ROCHE's excellent report completely clears up the state of the crater area. I wish to express my appreciation of the work in which Major ROCHE has worked whilst in charge of the crater area. He has given almost entirely without rest and has conveyed most valuable information." Sgd. E. PEREIRA Brig Gen Comdg 47th Bde	Map 36cNW.3 Edition 3
PHILOSOPHE 15th			Weather fine + cool. Casualties nil.	
BATT. in SUPPORT	16		We relieved 6th CONNAUGHT RANGERS in support in TENTH AVENUE from G 23 c. to G 17 to G 18 a to RESERVE TRENCH from G 17 G to G 24 b. D Coy going. Weather showery. Casualties nil.	
TENTH AVENUE	17		1 Officer + Batt found working parties of 40 men to remove chalk from our mines at H 13 a 2.9 and 1 officer & 18 men to clear the front line trenches near the same place where they had been almost choked with sand bags. Both then were permanent night + day parties. Casualties nil.	

Army Form C. 2118.

WAR DIARY
INTELLIGENCE SUMMARY.
(Erase heading not required.)

Place	Date	Hour	Summary of Events and Information	Remarks and references to Appendices
Batt: in support	April 1916			
	18th		Weather fine. Casualties 2 men wounded (accidentally shot) L-Cpl MULHALL of Reserve M.G. Section killed	
	19th		Night 19/20th very wet. Casualties 1 man killed, 5 men wounded	
	20		Relieved about 7 p.m by 8th ROYAL IRISH FUSILIERS Batt: left trench about 8 p.m and marched overland by PHILOSOPHE to NOEUX LES MINES where it went into billets for brigade rest. Weather showery	AMnD23

Army Form C. 2118.

WAR DIARY
or
INTELLIGENCE SUMMARY.

(Erase heading not required.)

Instructions regarding War Diaries and Intelligence Summaries are contained in F. S. Regs., Part II. and the Staff Manual respectively. Title pages will be prepared in manuscript.

Place	Date	Hour	Summary of Events and Information	Remarks and references to Appendices
NOEUX - LES-MINES	April 1916 21		Good Friday Church Parade. Weather wet	
"	22		Wet ~~during~~ all day	Annex3
"	23		Easter day Church Parade. Weather fine	
"	24		Fine. Batt firing on range + practising bombing	Annex3
"	25		ditto.	
"	26		ditto.	Annex3

Army Form C. 2118.

WAR DIARY
or
INTELLIGENCE SUMMARY.
(Erase heading not required.)

Place	Date	Hour	Summary of Events and Information	Remarks and references to Appendices
NOEUX-LES-MINES	April 1916 27		Battalion stood-to at 6.30 a.m on account of German gas attack between HULLUCH + PUITS 14 BIS, and was subsequently on half-an-hour notice to move	
	28		Advance party went up to take over trenches from 8th R.D.F. in left half of PUITS 14 BIS section arriving after dark.	
	29		Germans started sending over gas at 3am. It was almost on left company sector when C. by was, and Lt Kihill + 2nd Lt Horan who were there + 2nd Lt Foote who was in reserve time were gassed in spite of having helmets on. Gas began to clear off about 3.50 a.m. going back towards German lines. The Germans neither fired nor attacked. Our officers got on the parapet and the men were kept + shoulders over for two hours without being fired at. Casualties 2 NCOs died of gas 2nd Lt J.H.S. NIHILL 2nd Lt C.R. HORAN 2nd Lt G.B. FOOTE + 15 other ranks 1 man wounded. Batt arrived of took over time about 9.30.p.m	

Army Form C. 2118.

WAR DIARY
or
INTELLIGENCE SUMMARY.
(Erase heading not required.)

Place	Date	Hour	Summary of Events and Information	Remarks and references to Appendices
LEFT HALF PUITS 14 BIS SECTOR	April 30 1916		A B & C Companies in front line. D Coy in Reserve. Considerable interchange of rifle grenades, aerial torpedoes and trench mortar fire. Casualties Nil.	

Confidential
8th R. Muns. Fus.
WAR DIARY
or
INTELLIGENCE SUMMARY.

Army Form C. 2118.
8th R.M.F.
Vol 5

Place	Date	Hour	Summary of Events and Information	Remarks and references to Appendices
LEFT HALF PUITS 14 BIS SECTOR	Feby 1916 1		Trench mortar rifle grenade & aerial torpedo activity Weather fine Casualties 1 man killed 2 wounded	XVI
	2		Weather fine Casualties 5 men wounded	
	3		Weather fine Casualties 1 man killed 11 wounded	
	4		Weather fine Casualties 1 man killed	
	5		Weather fine Casualties 5 men wounded Same kind of enemy activity every day	

O.C. 8 R.M.F.

Army Form C. 2118.

WAR DIARY
or
INTELLIGENCE SUMMARY.
(Erase heading not required.)

8th R M F

Instructions regarding War Diaries and Intelligence Summaries are contained in F.S. Regs., Part II. and the Staff Manual respectively. Title pages will be prepared in manuscript.

Place	Date	Hour	Summary of Events and Information	Remarks and references to Appendices
LEFT HALF PUITS 14 B15	1916 May 6		There are very few dug outs in this section of line and battalion started making new ones morning quiet. Trench mortars & rifle grenades going in afternoon. Weather fine. Casualties 4 men wounded	
	7		Work done cleaning Bojano 8 & 9 which form the sides of MUNSTER STRONG POINT. Wiring done in front of this. Battalion was to have been relieved this evening but stayed on. Weather cooler. Casualties 1 man killed 2 wounded 1 of whom died next day	
	8		Enemy more active than recently with snipers & the usual grenades & trench-mortars especially about the anniv--- ing stand-to. 2nd Lt DODD, J.O.C. wounded Casualties 1 man killed 6 wounded	

#333 Wt. W2544/1454 700,000 5/15 D. D. & L. A.D.S.S./Forms/C. 2118.

Army Form C. 2118.

WAR DIARY
or
INTELLIGENCE SUMMARY.

8th R M F

Place	Date	Hour	Summary of Events and Information	Remarks and references to Appendices
LEFT HALF PUITS 14 BIS SECTOR	May 1916 9		Work done on LEINSTER STRONG POINT between Bayans 10 & 11. Weather cool. Usual Torpedoes & Grenades. Casualties L/Cpl 3253 Best killed and 4434 Pte BENNETT killed 4950 Pte Sarsfield P 5713 Pte CRONIN S. 3494 Pte RONAN P Wounded. 3299 Pte WALSH Wounded 3782 Pte McMAHON P J Missing	
	10		Little enemy activity with artillery, rifle grenades or torpedoes. at 1 a.m Lt BIGGANE went out to enemy's sap at H 25 d 4.9 It was unoccupied. He brought back two notice boards put up by the Germans with the following announcements:- (1) "Irishmen! Heavy uproar in Ireland; English zinn on fireny at your wifes and children! 1st May 1916" (2) "Interesting war-news of April 29th 1916. Kut el Amara has been taken by the Turks, and whole english army therein – 13000 men – maken prisonners." being army Major McCarey I/C mt for O.Comdg 8 R.M.F.	

WAR DIARY or INTELLIGENCE SUMMARY.

Army Form C. 2118.

8th R.M.F

Place	Date	Hour	Summary of Events and Information	Remarks and references to Appendices
LEFT HALF PUITS 14 BIS SECTOR	May 1916 10		Battalion was relieved about 11 p.m. by 7th LEINSTERS and marched to WEST PHILOSOPHE where it went into Hutts. 2nd Lt C R HORAN returned to duty. Casualties: 4399 Pte WALSH wounded and died next day; 3327 Pte DALY P. gunshot wound; 4879 Pte HUNT T.; 1301 Pte BOYLE J. 4207 Pte CLIFFORD wounded 4661 Cpl QUIGLEY J. gassed	
WEST PHILOSOPHE	11		Battalion resting in Reserve; furnishing large working parties every night to trenches in MENSTER STRONG POINT. Casualties 5832 Pte MULQUEEN J & 1339 Pte CONWAY J. wounded	
	12		PHILOSOPHE bombarded but not east of the railway	
	13		Nothing happened here. Col. WILLIAMSON & MAJOR ROCHE went on leave. Capt R H CRICHTON (O.C. B Coy.) left battalion going to 6th C.R.& [?]	

Army Form C. 2118.

8th RMF

WAR DIARY
or
INTELLIGENCE SUMMARY.
(Erase heading not required.)

Place	Date	Hour	Summary of Events and Information	Remarks and references to Appendices
PHILOSOPHE EAST	14/5/16		PUITS 3 heavily bombarded during evening and a few shells among our billets, one house being wrecked. Church parade held in morning. Casualty Pte 4234 WILSON S. wounded.	
"	15th		Working parties to front line every night. Lt. H. McCLARTY struck off strength of battalion & went to England.	
"	16th			
"	17th		Battalion relieved by 8th R. Irish. Fusiliers and went into huts at MAZINGARBE (south) for Brigade res. arriving there about 6.p.m. Enquiries from different companies show that only one man H in the battalion has so far been hit by a rifle bullet aimed at him in daylight since we have been in France.	

17/5/16 [signature] 8/R.MF

Army Form C. 2118.

8th R M F

WAR DIARY
INTELLIGENCE SUMMARY

Place	Date	Hour	Summary of Events and Information	Remarks and references to Appendices
MAZIN-GARBE (SOUTH)	18/5/16		Battalion bathing. All rifles inspected by Armourer Sergt. 2 Officers + 50 men from each company went to NOEUX LES MINES for presentation of their decorations by G O C 1st Army to Officers & men mostly of 1st Division	
"	19/5/16		Battalion kit inspections and all deficiencies indented for. Weather fine. Working parties at night. Capt J H HALL went on short leave. Gas Alert	
"	20th		200 men of battalion went into Divisional Cinema NOEUX LES MINES. Gas Alert	
"	21st		Church Parade. R C service in cemetery. Weather fine. Gas Alert. Officers not on duty went to Brigade gas lecture and test at NOEUX LES MINES	

Army Form C. 2118.

8th R M F

WAR DIARY
or
INTELLIGENCE SUMMARY
(Erase heading not required.)

Place	Date	Hour	Summary of Events and Information	Remarks and references to Appendices
MAZINGARBE (SOUTH)	22/5/16		Battalion practising bombing + shooting; and exercising in D P Gas helmets for at least 15 minutes. Some rain in evening. Gas alert cancelled. During morning Major O'BRIEN (for C.O) inspected kit of entire battalion. Batt: finished digging trenches # beside huts for shelter in case of bombardment. 2nd Lieuts T.J.O'MEARA and W.T. PHILLIPS arrived from 5th Batt. Bombing wiring + night patrolling practised.	
"	23		40 men per company and proportion from details went to Gas demonstration at VERQUIN	
"	24		Advance parties from battalion went up to take over trenches from 9th RDF arriving about 6 p.m. The Divisional Sector whose left word to be STONE STREET has been moved 1500 yards South. The battalion front is a left half of left sub sector and extends from VENDIN ALLEY H.19.a.4.2. to Boyau 62 H.25.b.3.2. being a total length of 1100 yards	

WAR DIARY
INTELLIGENCE SUMMARY
(Erase heading not required.)

Army Form C. 2118.

8th R.M.F

Place	Date	Hour	Summary of Events and Information	Remarks and references to Appendices
MAZINGARBE (SOUTH) 14 BIS LEFT HALF	25/5/16		Battalion left MAZINGARBE and marched to trenches described yesterday taking them over about 8 p.m. #6th R SCOTS FUS (15 Div.) were on our left and 6th ROYAL IRISH on our right. Our trench strength was 303. The night was quiet. Casualty Pte 3538 DUNDON M wounded.	
"	26		Enemy fairly quiet, sending over some aerial torpedoes & rifle grenades. We repaired our trenches when they had been damaged, and constructed shelters. Some hostile shelling on our front & support line during evening. Night quiet. 4 wiring parties out in front. Casualties killed L/Cpl 4455 LYNCH W 4771 Pte WALSH J. and 4461 Pte LILLIS. P. (all by one shrapnel) 3 Officers Patrols examined German wire & found it strong.	
"	27		A number of rifle grenades came over at dawn to which we retaliated. Day quiet. Batt was warned from above that there were signs of an intended German attack in the near future	signed illegible Major 8th RMF

Army Form C. 2118.

8th R.M.F.

WAR DIARY
or
INTELLIGENCE SUMMARY.
(Erase heading not required.)

Place	Date	Hour	Summary of Events and Information	Remarks and references to Appendices
14 BIS LEFT HALF	May 1916 27th		At 7.30 p.m. the evening being very calm, the enemy began to shout across to us in bad English. They were in such high spirits that it seems possible they were drunk. Casualties nil. Capt C J LAWKTREE went on leave. 3 Officers went out, and 3 Night quiet. wiring parties.	
"	28th		Day was quiet until 7.30 p.m when enemy heavily bombarded our front & support lines right of POSEN ALLEY. The ROYAL IRISH got more of it than we did. Our B Coy on the right got a good deal and D Coy some; C Coy were on the left & A Coy in reserve and they escaped. A copy of Gen. PEREIRA's circular on the subject is attached. Casualties Killed 3772 Pte O GORMAN D Wounded 3581 L-Ql LYNCH J. 4057 Pte MADIGAN J 5943 Pte MARTIN 5630 Pte BOURKE Night quiet. 2 Officer patrols + 1 NCO's patrols out 3 wiring parties out.	signed Major O.C. 8 R.M.F.

Army Form C. 2118.

8th R M F

WAR DIARY
or
INTELLIGENCE SUMMARY.
(Erase heading not required.)

Place	Date	Hour	Summary of Events and Information	Remarks and references to Appendices
14 B15 LEFT HALF	29/5/16		At 3.45 a.m RMunsB our artillery bombarded enemy's reserve trench opposite left of battalion with shrapnel until 5 a.m. There was slight retaliation on the Scotch to our left. At 4 p.m enemy opened a bombardment on C Coy front and support lines till 5.30 p.m doing little damage & causing few casualties. At 5.30 p.m Batt was relieved by 7th LEINSTERS and C & D Coys marched to PHILOSOPHE WEST where they went into RMunsB billets as Brigade reserve. A + B Coys stopped in TENTH AVENUE in view of expected attack. Then HQ at G.28.6.9.7 Casualties killed 4769 Pte SHEEHAM & 4117 L-Cpl SULLIVAN. Wounded (accidentally) 4272 Pte MURPHY	
PHILOSOPHE WEST G.13.d.a.5	30		C + D Coys resting + cleaning up A + B Coys in TENTH AVENUE. A draft of the following officers + 104 OR arrived from the 9th R. MUNS. FUS.	RMunsB

Army Form C. 2118.

8th R M F

WAR DIARY
or
INTELLIGENCE SUMMARY.
(Erase heading not required.)

Instructions regarding War Diaries and Intelligence Summaries are contained in F. S. Regs., Part II. and the Staff Manual respectively. Title pages will be prepared in manuscript.

Place	Date	Hour	Summary of Events and Information	Remarks and references to Appendices
PHILO-SOPHE WEST	30/5/16		Officers from 9th R M F taken on strength of 8th R M F Lt Col E MONTEAGLE-BROWNE took command of 8th R M F Major T. A. N. BOLTON Capt R A FRIZELLE Capt J C WATTS RUSSELL 1st Lt M F FITZGERALD 2nd Lt J F GLEESON 2nd Lt E HOLLAND 2nd Lt F CASEY 2nd Lt G ROCHE	
"	31st		CO inspected C & D Coys, the draft, MG section + bombers	

31-5-16

SECRET 47th Inf. Bde. No. 832/P.D.

Bombardment of 28th May, 1916.

At about 7.15 p.m. the enemy bombarded our trenches with heavy and light guns, combined with heavy trench mortars for about half an hour. They damaged some bays in the front and support trenches, chiefly near RAILWAY ALLEY and E of the Quarry, whilst one direct hit was obtained on FOREST TRENCH. Notwithstanding the intensity of the bombardment the casualties only amounted to 1 killed and 4 slightly wounded in the 6th Royal Irish Regt., who came under the heaviest bombardment, and 1 killed and 3 slightly wounded in the 8th Munsters.

The smallness of the casualties is to be attributed to the excellent discipline and coolness of the men, whilst it again proves that the actual loss of life from artillery fire for troops in trenches is small, and the effects of artillery are more moral than material.

The greatest praise is due to all ranks for their coolness under fire, the energy they displayed in repairing the damage at once, and it is to be regretted that opportunity did not present itself of meeting the enemy at close quarters, and showing what Irishmen can do in open and fair fighting.

We have to deal with a dispirited and skulking enemy, who is beginning to get pinched for food and who realizes that he is fighting a losing battle at the front, whilst his family is suffering the pangs of hunger at home.

His chief object is to protect himself, and for this purpose he has for a long time been working feverishly to cover his front with more and more wire, and to take refuge in dug-outs, whilst relying on the artillery or heavy trench mortars to fight for him. It is satisfactory to note that the shells being used by him now are dated 1916.

The following men of "C" Company 6th Royal Irish Regiment have been specially mentioned for very gallant conduct during the bombardment:-

No. 4836 Private J.S.BRYANT, a native of DUBLIN. During the bombardment he stood on the fire step, looked out for the heavy trench mortars and gave warning to his comrades.

No. 9837 L/Cpl. L.COMINO and No. 1900 Private T.BYRNE, during the bombardment they went out and repaired the telephone.

The names of these 3 men are being sent in to the higher authorities.

30th May, 1916.

G. Pereira
Brigadier-General,
Commanding The 47th Infantry Brigade.

Army Form C. 2118.

47/10

8th Royal Munster Fusiliers

WAR DIARY
INTELLIGENCE SUMMARY.
(Erase heading not required.)

Place	Date	Hour	Summary of Events and Information	Remarks and references to Appendices
PHILOSOPHE	1.6.16		The Coy. transferred from the to 9th Bn. proceeded on the Nunnery for inspection by Brigadier General Trevor C.H.G. D.S.O. who informed himself very pleased with the appearance of the men. "D" coy. 9 R.M.F. learn "D" Coy. of the 8th R.M.F. under the following officers: Capt. Hasell Capt. Walsh-Atkell, 2 Lt. Lyne Gleeson, is Sheehan. The original "D" Coy. 8th R.M.F. was divided between the other 3 coys. of the Battn. officers transferred from the 9th: Major T.N. Pelton + 2 Lts. Hallinan were posted to "B" coy. 2 Lt. Fitzgerald + another mistake [illeg.]	
TRENCHES BDE. SUP. PORT. PUITS 14 BIS SECTION.	2.6.16		The Bn. relieved the 6th Bn. Royal Irish Regiment in the Brigade Support line. PUITS 14 BIS SECTION. The Companies were disposed as follows: "D" coy. in RESERVE TRENCH, "C" coy. in GUN ALLEY, "A" & "B" coys. in 10th AVENUE & N. SAP REDOUBT.	
	3.6.16		The Bn. was employed on the usual work of Trench Maintenance, Repair, Carrying parties were found for 155 Coy. R.E. & the Brigade Bomb Store. There was some Shelling of WENDIN ALLEY & TENTH AVENUE which did no damage.	
	4.6.16		Work of Trench Maintenance was continued, Carrying parties as above. Damaged S.A.A. was cleared from H.11" heads in front of 10th AVENUE. A new loop trench was started in POSEN ALLEY where the W.N. had been lowered by shell fire. A very heavy artillery Bombardment of the enemy lines, in which field pieces mortars etc. took place in the early morning in support from [illeg.] enterprise carried out by 7th Division in the LEFT SUBSECTION on the extension of the writing of 9th May by W. Kay. the following honours were conferred on members of the Battalion :- Lr Colonel F. Montagu-Browne - D.S.O. ; Lt. H.M. Mitchell - Military Cross : No.9/4575 Pte Leahy + No.9/1729 Pte. Bailey - Military Medal.	

F Montagu Browne
Lr. Colonel.
Commd. 8th R.M.F.

Army Form C. 2118.

WAR DIARY
or
INTELLIGENCE SUMMARY.   8th Royal Munster Fusiliers

(Erase heading not required.)

Instructions regarding War Diaries and Intelligence Summaries are contained in F.S. Regs., Part II. and the Staff Manual respectively. Title pages will be prepared in manuscript.

Place	Date	Hour	Summary of Events and Information	Remarks and references to Appendices
TRENCHES BDE. SUP. PORT.	5.6.16		Work of Trench Maintenance continued. Carrying parties as above. The "T" heads in front of 10st AVENUE were organised for defence + a box of S.A.A. was placed in position in each the Bay.	M
PUITS 14 BIS SECTION	6.6.16		Work of Trench Maintenance continued. Carrying parties were found as above. A new dugout at Battalion Headquarters was completed. The Bn. relieved the 7th Leinster Regt. in the LEFT SUBSECTION PUITS 14 BIS SECTION. The companies were disposed as follows from Left to right in the from 15 up to 10 30 Lines "A" Coy. "B" Coy. "D" Coy. In Reserve; "C" Coy.	M
	7.6.16		The Bn. was employed clearing the communication trenches which were they had been knocked in by shell fire, reinforcing the parapets which were very thin in this Subsection, and strengthening the wire. Wiring parties were sent out by all companies in their own subsections. Officers patrols were sent out by all companies. One officer patrol discovered & an entanglement which had been half continued out 12 German General. He wander were killed and BOYAU 62 was hit by an open sortie. There were some exchanges of rifle grenades from Rupts coy. An enemy's working party in the enemy lines on their front until and obtain after the enemy put up a succession of Verey lights to the left of the S subsection. About 7.45 pm of their 8 bit a light about 36" apart which appeared to be connected. An enemy season some Shelling of 1904 AVENUE ensued.	M

F.M. Montagu Brodie
Lt. Colonel.
Commdg 8th R.M.F.

Army Form C. 2118.

WAR DIARY
or
INTELLIGENCE SUMMARY.

(Erase heading not required.)

8th Royal Munster Fusiliers

Place	Date	Hour	Summary of Events and Information	Remarks and references to Appendices
TRENCHES LEFT SUB SECTION PUITS 14 BIS SECTION	8.6.16		The work of Trench Maintenance was continued. All loose boards in the trench drain system were collected & cleaned. Wiring & gum cutting proceeded on all coy. fronts. Officers patrols were sent out by all coys. from 2.30 – 2.45 a.m. The enemy bombarded on trench with aerial torpedoes until they were silenced by our Stokes Mortars. During the afternoon our left company searched the enemy trenches on their front with rifle grenades, Stokes Mortars, & Heavy Trench Mortars, doing considerable damage. Shortly after, 5 m.m. an artillery retaliation on the enemy front line system did some excellent damage to his inspection Nt. Officers S.L.L. parties to explode.	
	9.6.16		The work of Trench Maintenance was continued. Addition of steps were constructed in SUPPORT LINE. S.A.A. was carefully released & damaged rounds salved. Wiring & gum cutting proceeded on all coy. fronts. There was considerable activity with Trench Mortars, Rifle Grenades, & Field artillery in all sections on both sides attentively. A medical dump was found 50 yds from the German wire & thought to be our open patrols. It was of the ordinary metal springs to the Prussian Army.	
	10.6.16		The work of Trench Maintenance was continued. About 3 a.m. our snipers accounted for a German at MAIDEN edge of POSEN CRATER, wounding him with the first shot. Relating with the third. The Bn. was relieved by the 6th Bn. Royal Inniskilling Fusiliers & marched to BILLETS at NOEUX LES MINES, when they arrived about 1 A.M. 11th inst. The spirits of the men were excellent. Casualties during tour of duty in Trenches from 2.6.16 – 10.6.16: Killed 2 OR Wounded: Capt. R.A. FRIZELL & 15 OR	

E Montagu Brade
Lt Colonel
Commdg. 8th R.M.F.

Army Form C. 2118.

WAR DIARY
or
INTELLIGENCE SUMMARY.   8th Royal Munster Fusiliers
(Erase heading not required.)

Instructions regarding War Diaries and Intelligence Summaries are contained in F. S. Regs., Part II. and the Staff Manual respectively. Title pages will be prepared in manuscript.

Place	Date	Hour	Summary of Events and Information	Remarks and references to Appendices
NOEUX-LES-MINES	11.6.16		The Battalion paraded for Divine Service at the Church at NOEUX at 11AM. The Companies were employed cleaning up their billets which had been handed over on a duty condition by the outgoing battalion. The Commanding officer went on leave to England. The Battalion was ordered to find a guard of N.C.O.s & men daily during their stay at NOEUX for Divisional Headquarters.	NT
	12.6.16		The Companies paraded for Bath & Change of underclothing at the Divisional Bath NOEUX. Major T.A. N. Bolton & 2.O.R. proceeded on leave. Rapid adjustment of Gas Helmets was practised by all Companies.	NT
	13.6.16		A Memorial Service for Field Marshall Earl Kitchener of Khartoum was held at the Y.M.C.A. Hut NOEUX at 11 A.M., when Last Post was blown by the Buglers of the Battalion. Major V.T. Kelly M/C NOEUX to proceed to the Base. Company Battalion Bombing & M.G. Sections. The Battalion Snipers paraded for Special Instruction under 2/Lt. Bieber, Pte Casey, Pte O'Brien. Running & Shooting in Gas Helmets was practiced by all Companies.	NT
	14.6.16		There was a Special performance Annual Extracts The Battalion at the Battalion Divisional Cinema NOEUX during the evening attended the G.O.C. 47th Bn. 15th Bn. presented Supplemental Certificates 15th Platoon. Pte. T. Greene, Capt. R.A. Ingall & 11166 Sgt. J. Burke. No. 5846 Pte. T. McDonough & No. 1669 Pte. 16th Divisional Provost Certified were unable to attend the Presentation through wounds. Training to on Yesterday The Battalion Wires were excellent in Wiring by night on 16th & only Regimental NOEUX from 5-11 pm The band played at dinner at 7 pm. Major W. McC. Crosbie joined the Battalion Capt. Hamilton returned from leave.	NT

F.W. FitzGerald, Major
Commanding 8th R.M.F.

WAR DIARY or INTELLIGENCE SUMMARY

Army Form C. 2118.

8th Royal Munster Fusiliers

Place	Date	Hour	Summary of Events and Information	Remarks and references to Appendices
NOEUX-LES-MINES	15.6.16		Trained as yesterday. The Battalion were received in right wing on Tuesday (Sunday) from 5-11 pm. A Reinforcement Draft of 19 O.R.s joined the Battalion. The Band played at Retreat at 7 pm. There was a lecture for all officers at H.Q. 47th Bde. at 5 pm. Subject: "Artillery". The following members of the Battalion were mentioned in despatches: Lt Colonel E Montagu-Bowen D.S.O., Major L. Roche.	
	16.6.16		There was a Conference at H.Q. 47th Inf. Bde. for Specialist Officers at 11 am. Bombing - 9 am: Signalling - 9.30 am: Sniping - 10 am. Training as on preceding days. There was a lecture for Battalion Lewis Gun holders early from 5 - 5.30 pm on "Wiring by Night". The Battalion paraded for Divine Service at 9 am. The Band played at Retreat at 7 pm.	
RIGHT SUB-SECTION LOOS SECTION	17.6.16		There was a Conference for Commanding Officers, 2 in Command, + Adjutants at H.Q. 47th Inf. Bde. at 9 am. The Battalion relieved the 9th Battalion Royal Dublin Fusiliers in the RIGHT SUBSECTION LOOS SECTION. The companies were disposed as follows: Right: A coy. Right Centre: C coy. Left centre: D coy. Left: B coy. The Battalion proceeded with the usual Trench Maintenance. Working parties Relief was sent out by all companies.	
	18.6.16		Trench Maintenance continued. The enemy displayed an abnormal activity with rifle grenades until silenced by our Stokes Mortars. An enemy aeroplane was observed to fall abruptly to the ground behind their line after an encounter with our own. Owing to the clearness of the night, our patrols could work in programme.	

E Montagu Bowen Lt Colonel
Command: 8th R.M.F.

Army Form C. 2118.

WAR DIARY
or
INTELLIGENCE SUMMARY. 8th Royal Munster Fusiliers
(Erase heading not required.)

Instructions regarding War Diaries and Intelligence Summaries are contained in F. S. Regs., Part II. and the Staff Manual respectively. Title pages will be prepared in manuscript.

Place	Date	Hour	Summary of Events and Information	Remarks and references to Appendices
RIGHT SUB-SECTION LOOS SECTION	19.6.16		Trench Maintenance continued. Patrols during night were sent out by all Coys. An officer patrol mostly about the GREEN MOUND. The enemy displayed considerable activity with Rifle Grenades, Torpedoes, Trench Mortars. We secured the ascendency of these. Our machine guns dispersed an enemy wiring party on our front.	JM
	20.6.16		Trench Maintenance continued. Patrols during night were sent out by all Coys. Enemy Snipers active. A man looking over the enemy parapet at M6.b.4.3. was shot by our Snipers. He is reported to have been young, dressed in a dark blue uniform, wearing a dark brown peakless cap with small circular white badge.	JM
	21.6.16		Trench Maintenance continued. Patrols during patrols were sent out only by all coys. A machine gun was discovered by one of our patrols in the enemy sap at M6.b.3.4. at 6.15 pm. The enemy opened on our front line with Artillery, Torpedoes, Rifle Grenades. The bombardment continued with the exception of a short lull until just after 8.30. The guns employed were 5.9". Our 4.9" howitzers retaliated with success. Between 11–12 midnight the Commanding officer returned from leave.	JM
	22.6/16		The Battalion relieved by the 7th Leinsters. Proceeded to BDE. SUPPORT — in which there disposed as follows. In the ENCLOSURE, B & D coys: in VILLAGE LINE & LENS ROAD REDOUBT, A coy; in DUKE STREET, C coy.	JM
	23.6.16		The Battalion found the following working & carrying parties: to 173rd Tunnelling Coy, 5 NCOs + 6 men; for 256 Tunnelling Coy, 8 NCOs + 80 men. The Companies proceeded with the usual work of Trench Maintenance in VILLAGE LINE + DUKE STREET. A reinforcing draft of 65 OR arrived. New duties to Companies. Between 8.45 – 9.10 p.m. the enemy opened a heavy bombardment after RIGHT SUBSECTION, which also extended to the Single Star, which when shattered the bombardment thereupon spread a number of lights, exciting the infantry on either flank our Rifles. During the latter stages of this fight the lights are such into their front green chain. An additional ...	JM

J. Murtagh Lt. Col.
Comdg 8 R.M.F.

Army Form C. 2118.

WAR DIARY
or
INTELLIGENCE SUMMARY. 8th Royal Munster Fusiliers
(Erase heading not required.)

Place	Date	Hour	Summary of Events and Information	Remarks and references to Appendices
BDE. SUP. PORT. LOOS SECTION	24.6.16		Working parties as yesterday. Work of Trench Maintenance continued on the Heavy Batteries were in action intermittently throughout the day. There was some rifle retaliation made from Pt q's & number of enemy Drift q on joined the Battalion from all its 4 Companies.	
	25.6.16		Working parties as yesterday. Work of Trench Maintenance & Salvage continued. An artillery & stokes mortar shelled the CRATER AREA IL to p.m. the day intermittently. About 3.45 pm. Some 20 tan aeroplanes flew over the enemy lines & dropped bombs which appeared the intending on his observation balloons. The balloons were drawn down rather approach. Bate fine the day F.H. hissness	
	26.6.16		Working parties as yesterday. Work of Trench Maintenance & Salvage continued. Between 9 & 10 AM the enemy shelled the VILLAGE LINE with field guns. About 5.35 AM the enemy sprang a mine at No 8. Sec 3. A party of our R.E. was found. No material damage was done. Between 3 & 4 p.m. the enemy opened a concentrated bombardment of the VILLAGE LINE around Battalion H.Q. with 4.2" guns.	
	27.6.16		Working parties as yesterday. Work of Trench Maintenance & Salvage continued. at 12.15 AM we sprang two mines in the CRATER AREA. On held from immediately searched the enemy front. & afterwards. Sounds of heavy working was heard. The enemy seemed slow in retaliating this fire. He retired beyond the RESERVE. An intense barrage against the enemies wire ? elements was usually stood two in progress.	
	28.6.16		The Battalion relieved the 7th Lenesters in WRIGHT SUBSECTION, LOOS SECTION. The Companies were disposed as follows: left: "D" Coy. Left centre: "C" Coy. Right Centre: A Coy. Right: B Coy. & draft of 66 OR. joined the Battalion at 1.15 AM. An artillery fired a very violent bombardment on the enemy defences sitting to his front line. It retaliated with severity on our Suffolk Ave. the CRASSIER, the ENCLOSURE, Reached our front line and Trench Mortar Rifle Grenade & Stokes mortar fire was kept up on our lines until 2.15. The day damaged our trench was down by HF then otherwise throughout the bombardment which lasted until 2.15. The day damaged our trench was down by HF enfilade fire from direction of WINGLES. Lt. Russell Comdy 8thR.M.F.

WAR DIARY or INTELLIGENCE SUMMARY

Army Form C. 2118.

Vol 6

8th Royal Munster Fusiliers

Place	Date	Hour	Summary of Events and Information	Remarks and references to Appendices
RIGHT SUB SECTION LOOS SECTION	29/6/16		Trench Maintenance continued. Patrols and wiring parties were sent out by all companies. Our artillery kept up slow & continuous fire during twilight. Our Stokes Mortars displayed working parties at NEW MOUND & on SAP E of HART'S CRATER, which had been invited by a patrol. A hun on M.G. Sprung on our right at 3 P.M. which was needed by our artillery. Our fire inflicted on our bullies, injured on enemy ammunition dump lying chief. Our patrols within the trees & Loos, we caught by enemy shell fire within the town & set on fire. The heads inflicted killed both horses & drivers. The enemy retaliated on two to a seven howitzers which kept firing twilight. Alternating them in several places. On butter artillery No. 3682 Cpl. P. Hogan lost his life in an attempt to bring in a wounded man in daylight from "O Horse Shoe" to "A" on Sappy M/C at 2.50 A.M. on enemy in conjunction with our Trench Mortars swept the enemy trenches with a burst of fire. Our field howh	
	30/6/16		Trench maintenance continued. Patrols & wiring parties were sent out by all Companies artillery in conjunction with our Trench Mortars swept the enemy trenches with a burst of fire. Our field howh recently cut over this line & fought have caused many casualties amongst enemy who would then have been stretchered. Ensures. A story officers patrol reconnoitred NEW MOUND N of HART'S CRATER. A large party working on the mound took flight before any capture could be effected. About 1.30 P.M. the enemy shelled Bn. HQ. in M.C. Loos with 4.2" + field guns.	

F.W. Westropp Blosse
Lt. Colonel
Commdg. 8th R.M.F.

Extract from Brigade Routine Orders dated 4.7.16. by Brigadier
General E. Pereira, C.M.G., D.S.O., Cmdg.
47th Infantry Brigade.

The G.O.C. 47th Infantry Brigade has much pleasure in publishing
the following letter which has been received from the G.O.C. 16th
Division and which will be communicated to all ranks:-

"Your Brigade has now come out of the line for a few
short days in Reserve. I wish to express to you and to all
ranks under your Command, my appreciation of the good work
which they have performed, especially during the last ten
strenuous days.

They have very nobly upheld the great traditions of the
Royal Irish and of Leinster Munster and Connaught.
I beg to convey to Colonels CURZON, LENNOX CONYNGHAM, BUCKLEY
and MONREAGLE-BROWNE, and to the Officers and men under their
Command my thanks for their unfailing cheerfulness under trying
conditions of weather and warfare, and my pride at the offen-
sive spirit which they have always shown. I know that those
will be maintained, and that your men will continue to be a
credit to the Irish Division and to the Land that gave them
birth."

Sd. W.B. HICKIE, Major General.
Cmdg. 16th Division.
Sd. F.V. THOMPSON, Major.
Bde. Major 47th Inf. Brigade.

"A" Form.
MESSAGES AND SIGNALS.

Army Form C. 2

Prefix	Code	m.	Words	Charge	This message is on a/c of:	Recd. at
Office of Origin and Service Instructions.			Sent		............Service.	Date......
			At.........m.			From......
			To........			
			By........		(Signature of "Franking Officer.")	By.......

TO — BLOATER

Sender's Number.	Day of Month	In reply to Number	
* M.C. 70	30th.		A A A

PATROL REPORT AAA During night a covering party went out between ROYAUX 37-38 and 1a in front of our line. The two parties were out for a period of two hours each and protected the damaged portion of trench. Very little work appeared to be done by the enemy on the right of HARTS CRATER and no wiring parties were out AAA

A strong officers patrol (LT. BIGGANE & LT. HORAN) went out on left of HARTS CRATER with the object of bringing in German prisoner. The party were showered by the enemy

From			
Place			
Time			

The above may be forwarded as now corrected.   (Z)

Censor.   Signature of Addressor or person authorised to telegraph in his name
* This line should be erased if not required.
(4198) Wt. W14042-M44. 300000 Pads. 12/15. Sir J. C. & S

"A" Form.
MESSAGES AND SIGNALS.

Prefix	Code	Words	Charge	This message is on a/c of:	Recd. at
Office of Origin and Service Instructions		Sent At ... m. To ... By ...		...........Service. (Signature of "Franking Officer.")	Date From By

TO

Sender's Number	Day of Month	In reply to Number	A A A

on the CRATER and fired upon. They were also seen of a party searching a NEW MOUND a rifle was taken river for the party to withdraw which was done before our party had time to approach them. On the return journey they bombed the ground between the CRATER and the MOUND a full account to be given with TACTICAL REPORT by LT HORAN

WIRE REPORT Work was carried as far as possible on the Chevaux de frise between BOYAUX 35-37. New wire added and strands fixed to ground ...

From
Place O.C. C. Coy.
Time

The above may be forwarded as now corrected. (Z)   D. Chandler Capt

Censor.   Signature of Addressor or person authorised to telegraph in his name
* This line should be erased if not required.

BLOATER

WAR DIARY

8th (S) Bn The
Royal Munster
Fusiliers

1st. July to 31st. July 1916.

VOLUME No. 8.

Army Form C. 2118.

WAR DIARY
or
INTELLIGENCE SUMMARY.
(Erase heading not required.)

Month: July
8th Royal Munster Fusiliers

Place	Date	Hour	Summary of Events and Information	Remarks and references to Appendices
RIGHT SUB- SECTION LOOS SECTION.	1.7.16		Tunnel maintenance continued. Our enemy patrols worked on the entanglements between BOYAUX 35 & 36 & at a SAP opposite BOYAU 39. Our Officers patrol reconnoitred the enemy SAP opposite LCRASSIER. Rifle Grenade & artillery activity was normal. Our snipers shot an officer enemy at the CRASSIER. The Battalion was relieved by the 7th Bn Leinster Regt. & proceeded to Bde Support in the VILLAGE LINE. The Companies were disposed as follows: in VILLAGE LINE A coy: in ENCLOSURE B & D Coys: in DUKE STREET C Coy. Of M.F.CASEY took over command of D Coy vice Capt J WATTS RUSSELL who proceeded to 1st Army School at BOULOGNE	
	2.7.16		The Battalion found 257 OR for Carrying parties for the R.E. & the Bde Bomb Store. The remainder were employed on Trench Maintenance. Sounds of heavy bombardment were heard from midnight on the right. Some searchlights were exposed by the enemy around PUITS 14 BIS. At 7.30 pm a column of dense black smoke went up from the direction of WINGLES & continues for over an hour. About 10.5 pm a barrage of shells was sent across from our line at PUITS 14 BIS & HULLUCH. The enemy immediately turned along his parapets some substance that glowed with a bright orange flame. Clearly the contour of his post as far northwards as NEUVE CHAPELLE. The situation appeared to become normal again by 11 pm. Capt. T.H. LAWLOR took over command of "A" Coy vice Major L. ROCHE who was admitted to hospital.	

J O'Brien Major
for Lt. Col
Comdg 8th Rl Munster Fus

Army Form C. 2118.

WAR DIARY
or
INTELLIGENCE SUMMARY.
(Erase heading not required.)

8th Royal Munster Fusiliers

July

Place	Date	Hour	Summary of Events and Information	Remarks and references to Appendices
BDE. SUP- PORT LOOS SECTION	3.7.16		The Battalion was relieved by the 7th Bn. Royal Innskilling Fusiliers Proceeded to Rest in the Huttments at MAZINGARBE Casualties during Tour of the Trenches from 17.6.16 to 3.7.16: Killed 2Lt. M.H. O'DONOVAN 2Lt. E.S. PROVIS + 30 O.R. Died of wounds: 4 O.R. Wounded: Capt. + adjt. T.E. SCOTT, Capt. C.J. LANKTREE J. HALL, 2Lt. F.J. BIGGANE, 2Lt. S.J. COBB, C.R. HORAN, P.T. LYNE, W + 123 O.R.	
MAZING- ARBE	4.7.16		The Battalion was employed cleaning kits + equipment. At 10 am the Commanding Officer inspected the Drafts that had joined the Battalion during the recent Tour of the trenches. The Band Played at Retreat at 6.30 pm	
	5.7.16		Tactically turning were practised by all coys. on the Bombay Ground MAZINGARBE. 2Lt. M.D. CREGAN was appointed Signalling Officer vice 2Lt. H.M. MITCHELL who returned to duty with A Coy. The Battalion found 2 officers + 232 O.R. for working parties	

Norman Mayer Lt Col.
Comdg. 8th Rl. Munster Fus.

Army Form C. 2118.

WAR DIARY
or
INTELLIGENCE SUMMARY.   8th Royal Munster Fusiliers
(Erase heading not required.)

Month: July

Place	Date	Hour	Summary of Events and Information	Remarks and references to Appendices
MAZINGARBE	6/7/16		The Battalion found the Same working parties as yesterday. All coys. paraded for Baths at the DIVISNL. BATHS MAZINGARBE. There was a working demonstration on the Bangalore Torpedo ground followed at 12.30 pm by a demonstration of the Bangalore Torpedo under the supervision of Lt. CASEY & 2Lt. BECHER. The Battalion marched to NOEUX LES MINES to attend a Special performance at the 16th DIVISNL. CINEMA at 5.15 pm during which the G.O.C. 47th INF. BDE presented Parchment Certificates for Gallantry to the following officer, NCOs & men of the Battalion; Capt. J.H. LAWLOR, 9/808 C.S.M. P. WILLIAMS, 8/978 Sergt. W. GIBBINS, 8/3821 Sergt. T. MORAN, 8/2770 Cpl. D. FLYNN, 9/1334 Pte. T. McDAID. Lt. MITCHELL + 3 OR proceeded to 16th DIVISN SCHOOL for a Course of instruction in Bombing. The G.O.C 16th DIVISION inspected the Battalion on its march to NOEUX LES MINES	
	7/7/16		The Battalion found the Same working parties as yesterday. 30 OR per Coy. together with details from the Transport & Quartermaster Stores marched to VERQUIN under the Command of Lt. CREGAN & 2 Lt. O'MEARA to attend a demonstration of Poison Gas. 2 Lt. WATTS proceeded on leave to England. A reinforcing draft of 2 OR arriving were posted to D Coy.	

J. J. O'Brien Major for Lt. Col.
Comdg. 8th Bn. Munster Fus

Army Form C. 2118.

WAR DIARY
or
INTELLIGENCE SUMMARY.

(Erase heading not required.)

8th Royal Munster Fusiliers

July

Place	Date	Hour	Summary of Events and Information	Remarks and references to Appendices
MAZING-ARBE	8.7.16		The Coy paraded for C.O's kit inspection, & to exercise in Racking wiring. The Battalion found parties to take number C/A of men & 168 ORR for to inspect & carrying empty Gas Cylinders from POICE La Bis Return under the Command Major O'BRIEN.	
	9.7.16		The Battalion paraded for Divine Service in the CEMETRY MAZINGARBE at 9am. The same carrying parties were found as yesterday. There was a conference of all Specialist officers at BDE. H.Q. NOEUX LES MINES which was attended by the Signalling, Scouting, Machine gun officers of the Battalion. The enemy shelled HAZINGARBE at 11am. A few 77m and 4.2" & 5.9" guns. The shells fell chiefly on the NOEUX – BRÉBIS Crossroad and around the Church. There were no casualties in the Battalion. J.E.A. OAKSHOTT, recovered from hospital & was posted to C Coy.	
	10.7.16		The Battalion found the Same company parties as yesterday. The Coys were exercised in Reading trench work, & in the rapid equipment for hostile.	

Mansur Major for Lt Col
Comdg 8th Rl Munster Fus.

Army Form C. 2118.

WAR DIARY
or
INTELLIGENCE SUMMARY.
(Erase heading not required.)

8th Royal Munster Fusiliers

July

Place	Date	Hour	Summary of Events and Information	Remarks and references to Appendices
PHILOSOPHE W BDE. RES- ERVE	11/7/16		The Battalion relieved 1st/4th Royal Munster Fusiliers in Bde Reserve Billets at PHILOSOPHE. 2Lt. J. FITZPATRICK & 6 OR proceeded to NOEUX to attend a course of Instruction at the XI Bd Machine Gun School. Carrying parties of 54 OR were found. 2Lt. MITCHELL & 4 OR reported from 16th DIVISN SCHOOL.	
	12/7/16		The Coy. proceeded to close order drill. 2Lt. SGO Kelner Inspection. A carrying party of 2 officers & 129 OR was found for the purpose of carrying sandbags for cylinders & their implements to PUITS 14 BIS Section.	
	13/7/16		Carrying party of 4 officers & 322 OR was found for same work as yesterday. Raiding parties of 30 men had coy. together with 1st Battalion Border carried out a Practice Raid after dark on a pit ground marked out for the purpose near the CHALK PIT at PHILOSOPHE, under the direction of Major CROSBIE.	

H. J. O'Brien Major
for Lt. Col.
Commdg 8th Rl. Munster Fus.

Army Form C. 2118.

WAR DIARY
or
INTELLIGENCE SUMMARY.
(Erase heading not required.)

8th Battalion Royal Munster Fusiliers

July

Place	Date	Hour	Summary of Events and Information	Remarks and references to Appendices
PHILOSOPHE W. BDE. RESERVE	14/7/16		Company parties at Yutkery. In honor of the national festival offr had to send Mayor Marseillaise at Retreat. A demonstration of Raiding was carried out & the duties under the direction of Major CROSBIE in presence of the G.O.C. 47th Bde.	
PHILOSOPHE PUITS 14 BIS	15/7/16	8.30 AM	The companies paraded for Divine Service in the Church PHILOSOPHE W at 8.30 AM. The commanding officer inspected steel helmets of all companies on parade at 10 AM. The Battalion relieved the 7th Devon Regt in Left Subsection PUITS 14 BIS after the Relief the Coys were disposed as follows: Left Coy represented by the 4 Raiding parties undertaken our officers with Capt. TEAM in O.P. Coy. Centre Coy C Coy. Right Coy: D Coy Reserve Coy: B Coy. It was Coy had hand grenade impressed by the aide mechanics for A Coy of the Raiding Parties which took over that part of the line from which they were about to start with the Right Platoon of "A" Covering themselves with the enemies wire there at our own posts. Patrols from the raiding parties examined the state of the enemy obstacles.	Mosrien major for Lt. Col. Comdg. 8th Bn Rl Munster Fus.

Army Form C. 2118.

WAR DIARY
or
INTELLIGENCE SUMMARY.
(Erase heading not required.)

8th Royal Munster Fusiliers

Instructions regarding War Diaries and Intelligence Summaries are contained in F. S. Regs., Part II. and the Staff Manual respectively. Title pages will be prepared in manuscript.

July.

Place	Date	Hour	Summary of Events and Information	Remarks and references to Appendices
POTIJZE B15	14/7/16		Work of Trench maintenance continued. Normal Rifle & Grenade & French Mortar activity. Taking from Ruislip huts reconnoitred the ground & the enemy entanglement on their fronts. One officer under command of Lt. MITCHELL brought in a German rifle & three equipment complete from a good deal of investigation from NO MAN'S LAND. The enemy has shown but very little reply on our front.	
	17/7/16	Work of Trench Maintenance continued. Patrols of the enemy who endeavoured to work on his wire opposite CRAB 63 & 45 & POSEN CRATER were dispersed by our Machine guns. Patrols from the Ruislip Huts reconnoitred the respective routes across to NO MAN'S LAND. Normal Rifle & Grenade & French Mortar activity. During the afternoon our artillery bombarded the enemy line at the S.O.S.	
	18/7/16	Work of Trench Maintenance Continued. During the day our artillery bombarded the enemy front line Osterx continuously, probably some French Mortar Retaliation. An enemy working party S. of POSEN CRATER was dispersed by our Machine guns.	

[signature] Major for L.C.
Comdg. 8th Rl. Munster Fus.

WAR DIARY or INTELLIGENCE SUMMARY

Army Form C. 2118.

5th Royal Munster Fusiliers

Place	Date	Hour	Summary of Events and Information	Remarks and references to Appendices
PUITS BIS.	14/7/16		At 12.30 AM. a series of 4 raids with French Mortar artillery co-operation was carried out on the enemy's line between BOYAUX X 9 & X 13. The parties consisted of 1 Officer & 29 OR. Each were divided as follows. Left party under Lt. MITCHELL 5th Co with a party with Lt. WOODLEY. Right Centre C party under 2/Lt. OBRIEN; Right D party with Capt CASEY. The Battalion Bombers in two parties X & Y under 2/Lt. BECHER supported the enterprise on the flanks at BOY/AU X 13 & BOYAU X 9 respectively. The 4 Bomber attack parties were covered by repeated salvos of "flying pineapples" direct from "No Mans Land," W on the enemy front line trenches. Owing to the late of McBaugh Torpedoes which were had hopert ready. None of the enemy were eopenento. Any attempt His Trench was unrealed. Instead our bombers threw from the parapet into the Trench assisted by hung candles. Our losses were Capt M F CASEY who was killed whilst attempting to rush the path in the enemy wire at the head of his Coy. 2/Lt E. R. F. BECHER and Lt. FURNEY Lt. N. V. O'BRIEN 1 OR Killed & 7 OR wounded. The Lewis Gun Section under Lt. FURNEY by means of advanced fire positions in NOMANS LAND engaged & silenced at 75 yds range an enemy Machine Gun that attempted to enfilade the retirement. 2/Lt H.N.V. O'BRIEN took over command of D Coy vice CAPT. M.F. CASEY. Killed in action. All casualties were recovered. The command of the Battalion was taken by Major Klang. In Lt.Col. CASEY from the enemy wire.	

Major O.C. the Munster Fus.

Munster Fus.

Army Form C. 2118.

WAR DIARY
or
INTELLIGENCE SUMMARY.
(Erase heading not required.)

8th Royal Munster Fusiliers

Place	Date	Hour	Summary of Events and Information	Remarks and references to Appendices
PUITS 14 BIS.	20.9.16		Following an intense bombardment at 11.50 p.m. 19th inst. which lasted 3 minutes A.B. & D parties again left their trenches to raid the enemy line on our left corp front — 2nd Lty Scout was under Command of 2/Lt. G.F MAHER. On [?] the enterprise was covered by apparatus Salvos of 12h grenades. A & B parties again failed to penetrate the enemy wire, but element of the front behind it will [?]. C party under Lt. O'BRIEN proceeded into the foe trench near BOXAU x 10 stumbled & successfully bombed BOXAU x 11. All dug outs that were bombers & a party of the enemy driven off into BOXAU Party D under 2 Lt. MAHER reached the enemy front trench near BOXAU 9 who had taken cover under a Roller were killed. The party then worked westwards inflicting several other Casualties, until the Captain became too Stiff with he they withdraws. The party were joined of Queen MULLIGAN's & on returning to [?] train on a fire will the enemy had by the [?] into a bombarded between [?] the [?] in the entanglement. An officer STEMLER himself to so up the section behind C Party but wounded this A.Co. with his revolver after he [?] and been assisted to his shop. A prisoner taken by D party & [?] endeavour & to break away from [?] an escort while passing through the enemy wire was Shot. Casualties [?] 5 Slightly	

Yerosnin Major fr. Lt. Col.
Comdg 8th Bn. Munster Fus.

Army Form C. 2118.

WAR DIARY
or
INTELLIGENCE SUMMARY.
(Erase heading not required.)

Title pages July
8th Royal Munster Fusiliers

Place	Date	Hour	Summary of Events and Information	Remarks and references to Appendices
PUITS 14	20/7/16		Killed 8 & 23 OR wounded. Officer 2 being killed & 5 wounded in attempt to sent prisoners to our lines. O/C enemy 2d in charge on officer in party have been killed by the enemy party in addition to casualties inflicted by artillery, rifle grenade & much Mortar fire. The battalion was relieved by the 7th Bn Leinster Rifles. Proceeded to Wells.	
at PHILOSOPHE W.			The following telegram was received from 47th Inf. Bde commander to all ranks: "SCA 309, 20.7.16 - Following from General W B Hickie began AAA Please convey to Colonel MONTEAGLE-BROWNE & men of 8th ROYAL MUNSTER FUSILIERS my appreciation of the veneer gallant night action & prise of their performance." S. F. HARRISON Capt. Staff Capt. 47th Inf. Bde. To Lt Rutynop The following message was despatched - Congratulations thank 8th MUNSTERS AAA Upon withdrawal from the excellent success gained & been fully & economically carried out on lies SV seen in night MSZA Commandy 8 MUNSTERS. Sd. E MONTEAGLE-BROWNE Lt Col Cmdg 8th Bn R M F	Morris Major for Lt Col. Comdg. 8th Bn Munster Fus

Army Form C. 2118.

WAR DIARY
or
INTELLIGENCE SUMMARY.
(Erase heading not required.)

8th Royal Munster Fusiliers

Place	Date	Hour	Summary of Events and Information	Remarks and references to Appendices
PHILOS-OPHE W	21.7.16		Capt M.P. CASEY, 2nd Lt E.R.F. BECHER + 5 OR who had been killed in the recent raids were buried with full military honors in the cemetery at MAZINGARBE. The funeral was attended by the G.O.C. 47th Bde & the representatives from all Corps of the Battalion. The G.O.C. 16th Division + G.O.C. 47th Bde Inf. Bde inspected & addressed parties of the Battalion & Workers outside the Nunnery at PHILOSOPHE. Rechecked letters were postage. Killed: Capt I A LAWLOR 503 CSM Collins. 805 CQMS Williams, 910 Sgt W Gibbons 3853 A/SM Ellis 3601 L/Cpl Dooley. 3389 SKEGRAN, 4334 Pte Baird, 3817 Pte Allison. Wounded 1 Officer + 12 5 OR for general duties 10 RE 1 Slightly at duty. Signallers Officers + 1 Suffered the Hospitals Station. The Band played at retreat at 6 p.m.	
	22.7.16			
	23.7.16		"A" Coy handed for Browne Sown at the Nunnery + Allan + Roman Catholics Div 9 a.m. Church of England at 11.45 a.m. Working parties were found as on Friday. The Band played at retreat at 6 p.m. The Medical Officer Lt. F.T. MURPHY was relieved by Lt. W. MARSHALL + proceeded to Ireland on leave.	

J.F. Stevenson Major for Lt. Col.
Comdg. 8th Bn Rl Munster Fus.

WAR DIARY
or
INTELLIGENCE SUMMARY.
(Erase heading not required.)

Army Form C. 2118.

5th Royal Munster Fusiliers

July

Place	Date	Hour	Summary of Events and Information	Remarks and references to Appendices
PHILOSOPHE	24/7/16		The Battalion found working parties as on yesterday. During the afternoon some 5.9 shells were fired into VERMELLES. The band played at retreat at 5 pm	
	25/7/16		The Battalion found working parties as above. The band plays at retreat at 6 pm. On the occasion of the presentation of His Majesty King [G?] to Col. M Williamson of the Victoria Cross for the encouragement at DUJAILIS on 10th April 1916 the Battalion His Majesty commanded Colonel Williamson to convey to all ranks his appreciation of their loyalty, gallantry & hard work, in terms on the plea sent for service to our losses and the attendants intends and which he has followed. "Allow our career the happily added; the oft repeated pattern of the Munsters. Colonel Williamson will now be forgotten by he on those who follow he."	
	26/7/16		The Battalion relieved the 9th R Inniskg Regt in left section right B15 after relief the coy were dispersed as follows Left A coy Centre C coy Right B coy in Reserve D coy Relief was not out by 11 all coys Rel by M.	

W.O'Brien Major for Lt-Col
8th Rl Munster Fus.

Army Form C. 2118.

WAR DIARY
or
INTELLIGENCE SUMMARY.
(Erase heading not required.)

8th Royal Munster Fusiliers

Place	Date	Hour	Summary of Events and Information	Remarks and references to Appendices
PONTS			July	
14 BIS	26/7/16		Lights were sent up about 9 pm from enemy Support line. A screen of wire was afterwards put up & was established in shell holes on our right half coy front.	
	27/7/16		Work of Trench Maintenance Continued. During the day enemy Heavy Trench Mortars shelled POSEN ALLEY & the SUPPORT LINE at that part of our line. Our wire was retaliated adequately. At 9pm a loud explosion was heard in the enemy line off Hook Box 63 and debris was thrown up, in the vicinity of our Stoke Heavy Trench Mortar emplacements. Enemy trying rifle & M/G at POSEN CRATER & at the KINK were dispersed by our Machine Guns. Patrols were sent out by all coys	
	28/7/16		At 11.40 PM the right Coy's Coy's Supported by artillery (Trench Mortars carried out an interprise) against the enemy on their front. The idea the scheme was to discover by means of a fresh artillery arrangement killed Major VJ Ryan whether there an attack was imminent on their front & to affix identity. Ho a cutting out party on the right under 2nd Lt. HOLLAND Reached Mann M Comdg. 8th Bn Munster Fus. J Norman major for Lt Col Comdg. 8th Bn Munster Fus	

Army Form C. 2118.

WAR DIARY
or
INTELLIGENCE SUMMARY.
(Erase heading not required.)

Title pages July   5th Royal Munster Fusiliers

Place	Date	Hour	Summary of Events and Information	Remarks and references to Appendices
PONS 14 BIS	29/7/16		The left party however of Carrier officers were intended to push home the attack. The Rangers together with parts now sent to an aperture of the enemy ahead on the front between parts 20 & 21 of the ridge. Engineer stores took with them leaving on him had when to the Lt. led this up through LLS was (under Lt. Kavanagh) then from run front. [struck out] 2 party then attempted to reach Lt. MITCHELL having been slightly wounded. The Right party were able to clean trenches from up through down & from Lt. Pelly & that was X 19. So the party had by 2 Lt. HOLLAND received his trench, and they found strongly held. The remainder of the party bombed the trench side for some length. They now had. Meanwhile 2 Lt. HOLLAND killed & all every one in turn. & cleared it finding the want of bombs failed & to fell the whole of Canal to both parts were Lt. MITCHELL & 7 O.R. wounded. All enemy seen killed in their own trench. 2/Lt. HOLLANDS party unknown of the bodies began after Enemy's artillery & trench mortars which had been seen.	

Mission major for H. Col.
County 6th Rl. Munster Fus.

Army Form C. 2118.

WAR DIARY
or
INTELLIGENCE SUMMARY.
(Erase heading not required.)

8th Royal Munster Fusiliers

Place	Date	Hour	Summary of Events and Information	Remarks and references to Appendices
PUITS 14 BIS.	29/7/16		The Battalion carried out a raid on the enemy front at 11.25 pm after 4 & 1/2 hours bomb. After 3 hours intense bomb. bombardment of the enemy front x9 & x 11 a Coy handed 4 artillery treatment of the enemy front 11.25 pm and they were known in NO MANS LAND on the post about 11 p.m. from a raid. W/. Lt Ryan found portion direct of the enemy wire & support in cheval so they did not go further but a while so immediately the artillery Switched to P.Sx trenches from x 16 GREEN CRATER & together with the SIRS trustees in the Eighty heavy trench Mortars withdrew. The raiders fired shots and brought 1 bomb home. 2/Lt FitzPatrick who brought party to clear Sap x2 + x3 a this moment to attack 4th machine emplacement at Sap x 1 + a shell hit party under 2/Lt HOLLAND & gave one early throat. He hit gunless x 11 x2 xs The whole party was now well supporting behind in fire + smoke ii x3 Enz. Patrick + 1 OR killed + 2 OR wounded + 5 or whether known of Germans of they lay the machine gun were known to us + killed. The whole party was then withdrawn. The enemy continued to the fire last for an hour and started to enemy splash between x2 + x3 Jt Highfull	Monday 8 & RLl Munster Fus.

T 2134. Wt. W708-776. 500000. 4/15. Sir J. C. & S.

Army Form C. 2118.

WAR DIARY
or
INTELLIGENCE SUMMARY.
(Erase heading not required.)

5th Royal Munster Fusiliers

July

Place	Date	Hour	Summary of Events and Information	Remarks and references to Appendices
PUITS 14 BIS	29/7/16		LANDS party moved into the enemy trenches & what is thought was though Kemp. It had been blown in thoroughly. The party worked without hindrance from enemy shewing upon them into the enemy's trenches by the Crater group in the parapet between x.2, x.3, x Crater (all dugouts were empty) & on the parapets an unwounded prisoner gave himself up & was escorted from line. The man belonging to v. Sturmn Regt. 5th Division. Report. An 18 year group was strong built and eighteen feet he had been 11 days front until the of 19 month. He said that the chain was protected acted as an outpost & that 5 deep. No Causalities were killed. Fitzpatrick, Q1 Q2 wounded 2nd Holland 16 Q.R. O/R. During the 25 were killed by the Enemy party alone 10th Sept. Thoroughly the 15th in addition much is indebted to Company Sergt. A. Roach & the Trench Major W. Mr. E. CROSBIE organized supplies of material for the recent party. Major T.A.N. Bolton acted as O.C. interprise	

M.J.O'Brien Major for Lt. Col.
Commdg 8 th Rl. Munster Fus.

Army Form C. 2118.

WAR DIARY
or
INTELLIGENCE SUMMARY.
(Erase heading not required.)

8th Royal Munster Fusiliers

Place	Date	Hour	Summary of Events and Information	Remarks and references to Appendices
PHILOSOPHE & BIS	30.7.16		Work of Trench Maintenance continued. The enemy Trench Mortars were active until silenced by our Artillery. On some exchanges Rifle Grenades, when our Artillery, the Artillery shewed how powerful it could be when hostility got to power 63. Enemy minning parties at several places on our front were dispersed by Lewis Guns.	
	31.7.16		The Battalion was relieved in left Subsector PHILOSOPHE & BIS by 8th Bn Royal Inniskilling Fusiliers, & proceeded by Battn to Huttments at NOEUX LES MINES. 2Lt FITZPATRICK was hurt and fell - Lt Withers however in command. MAZINGARBE. Casualties during from 9th March 11.7.16 — 31.7.16. Killed. Capt. M.F. CASEY, 2Lt T.J. FITZPATRICK, 4 15 O.R. Died of wounds 2 Lt E.R.F. BECHER: Wounded Lt Col. J.H. E MONTEAGLE-BROWNE (at duty), Lt H.N. MITCHELL, 2Lt E. HOLLAND, 4 100 O.R. P.S.D (at duty). Lt H.N. MITCHELL, 2Lt E. HOLLAND, 4 100 O.R. Died (in hospital not them) 2Lt S. COBB	

J J O'Brien Major
for Lt Col
Comdg 8th Bn R Munster Fus.
2/8/16

Appendix A

Copy No. _____

O R D E R S. 8th (S) Bn. The Royal Munster Fusiliers.

1. The Battalion will carry out a Raid on the Right Front of the Left Sub-Section, 14 Bde, on the night of 29th July 1916, from N.25.B.5.6. to N.25.B.5.4½ assisted by a strong demonstration of the Left Front of this Sub-Section, from N.19.C.9.6. to N.19.A.9.0.

2. The aim of the Operation will be to achieve the objects outlined for yesterday's raid and it will continue till this has been done.

3. Sequence of Events:

   Zero Time – An intense Stokes bombardment will be opened on
   (11-25pm)   the enemy front line from K9 to K11 lasting three
                minutes combined with a fire of one Battery R.F.A.
                on positions in rear.

   11-28 p.m. – Rockets will be sent up from "NO MAN'S LAND" and
                loud cheers raised by the Left Company who will
                open a vigorous grenade fire on the enemy line
                between K8 and K12 Hales grenades being used on
                the front line and Newton Grenades on the Support.
                At the same time the Stokes Mortars will lift to
                the Support.

   11-31 p.m. – A box barrage will be established by the Artillery
                from Y.16 to POSEN CRATER and will engage "OLGA
                MINENWERFER" while Stokes Mortars will engage
                "WINIFRED MINENWERFER" and also the rear of POSEN
                CRATER.

   The firing of the first shell at 11-25 p.m. will be the signal for the Stokes Mortars to open their bombardment. The rockets will be the signal for the Stokes Mortars to lift to the Support Line and the rifle grenading to begin. Colour of rockets will be given later.

4. The rifle grenaders will sustain their bombardment between K8 and K12 until the conclusion of the enterprise thereby inflicting heavy casualties on any of the enemy manning their line on that part of the front.

5. (i) On the opening of the barrage at 11-31 p.m. a party with the bangalore torpedo which will be in position between K2 and K3 will move forward and insert their torpedo in the wire. At the same time bombing parties on their flanks consisting of 1 N.C.O. and 4 men each will bomb along Saps K2 and K3 from inner sides and withdraw with the torpedo party when the torpedo has been placed in position. The torpedo will then be detonated and the torpedo party, the two bombing groups, and a further group of five raiders who will also carry mats, will rush forward. The bombing groups will then bomb from the parapet until the mats have been laid and an entry has been effected when they will follow into the trench.

   (ii) Simultaneously another party of 1 N.C.O. and 4 men will bomb the Machine Gun in Sap K1, attacking from the Southern side.

   (iii) A blocking party of 10 raiders will force an entrance between K1 and K2 by the gap made by the previous raid and carry out the task assigned by the Operation Order of the 28th instant.

The Raiding Parties will be under the Command of Lieuts. Holland and Fitzpatrick.

Major T.A.W. Bolton will act as O.C. Enterprise.

Major Volkn? Crozzie will be available at "B" Coy's Hd. Qrs. for all questions relating to Pierce?

5. **Machine Guns.** A Machine Gun will be in position in "NO MAN'S LAND" which, with the support of another Machine Gun situated in the front line will sweep the enemy parapet from 14 to ????.

7. **Communication.** Communication will be opened at Zero Time by all Coys. Touch will be maintained with the Raiders by means of a Telephone Buzzer and Operator who will take up position in a small sap in "NO MAN'S LAND" from which a close view of the operation may be obtained and communicated to Advanced Battalion Head Quarters at "B" Coy's Hd. Qrs in the support Line between Squares 64 and 65 where the Commanding Officer will be available.

8. A Red and a Green rocket fired simultaneously from "B" Coy's front will show that one at least of the parties has entered the enemy trench.

9. In anticipation of heavy artillery retaliation all ranks in front and support lines will take the best possible cover but will hold themselves in readiness to man their fighting positions immediately if an emergency should arise.

10. **Recall Signal.** There will be no Recall Signal so as every opportunity may be given to the raiding party to achieve its objects.

CRITICAL TIME. All Officers concerned will be particular to have their watches synchronised with Brigade Signal Time.

                                                    Lieut. Colonel.
                                        Cmdg 8th (S) Bn. Royal Munster Fusiliers.

Copy No. 1. -	Retained.	Copy No. 9. -	Major Bolton.
Copy No. 2. -	"A" Coy.	Copy No. 10. -	47th T.M.B.
Copy No. 3. -	"B" Coy.	Copy No. 11. -	47th M.G.C.
Copy No. 4. -	"C" Coy.	Copy No. 12. -	47th I. Bde.
Copy No. 5. -	"D" Coy.	Copy No. 13. -	O.C. L. Grp. A'ty.
Copy No. 6. -	Lt. Holland.	Copy No. 14. -	O.C. Rt. Bn. 14 Bde.
Copy No. 7. -	Lt. Fitzpatrick.	Copy No. 15. -	-do- BULLIOH.
Copy No. 8. -	M.G.O.	Copy No. 16. -	Bn. Sig. Offr.
		Copy No. 17.-M.G.O. i/c Bombers	
		Copy No. 18.-20 Retained.	

APPENDIX B. 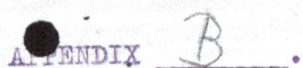   SECRET.

Copy No. 1. - A.77   Copy No. 8. - B.77   )
Copy No. 2. - A.177   Copy No. 9. - D.177   )
Copy No. 3. - B.177   Copy No. 10. - C.180   ) For Information.
Copy No. 4. - C.177   Copy No. 11. - D.180   )
Copy No. 5. - 47 I. Bde.   Copy No. 12. - 16 D.A.-
Copy No. 6. - Lt. McAlister.   Copy No. 13. - Retained.
Copy No. 7. - O.C. 8th Munsters. Copy No. 14. - Retained.

The 47th Inf. Bde. will carry out a Raid in the 14 BIS Sector to-night 29/30th July for the purpose of obtaining identifications.

1. Zero Time will be at 11-25 p.m. If it is necessary to alter Zero Time the message "RETARD X MINUTES" or "ADVANCE X MINUTES" will be sent. Brigade time will be sent round at 10-30 p.m.

2. At 11-25 p.m. A77 will engage Support Trench H.19.D.10.90 to H.19.D.13.60: rate of fire XF 5". H.E. will be used.
   At 11-31 p.m. fire will cease and the battery will relay on night lines and break off.

3. At 11-31 p.m. B177, C177 and A177 will open fire on the following objectives:-
   A.177 - C.T. H.25.B.74.10 to H.25.B.90.40.
   B.177 - Support Trench H.25.B.75.70 to trench junction
           H.25.B.80.45.
   C.177 (1 section) - POSEN CRATER and front trench to
                       H.19.D.28.15.
    -do- (1 section) - H.19.D.28.15 to trench junction H.19.D.49.26.

   Rate of fire - 11.31 p.m. - 11-33 p.m. - XF 5"
                  11.33 ,, - 11-38 ,,   - XF 10"
                  11-38 ,, - "ALL IN"   - XF 20"

   A.177 and B.177 and the section of C.177 firing on front trench will fire AX and the section of C.177 firing on C.T. will fire A.

4. On receipt of the message "O'GRADY IN" batteries will slow down to a rate of XF 10" and B.177 will at once lift on to C.T. H.25.B.80.45. to H.25.B.99.57 and fire shrapnel.

5. On receipt of the message "QUICKEN" batteries will double their rate of fire.

6. On receipt of the message "ALL IN" batteries will stop firing and stand by.

7. On receipt of the message "SITUATION NORMAL" batteries will relay on night lines and break off.

8. ACKNOWLEDGE.

                                    Sd. R.J. Jobson, Lieutenant, R.F.A.,
29/7/16.   Adjutant, RIGHT GROUP.

Vol 8

WAR DIARY.

8th Royal Munster Fusiliers

MONTH OF AUGUST, 1916.

VOLUME:- 9

Army Form C. 2118.

WAR DIARY
or
INTELLIGENCE SUMMARY.
(Erase heading not required.)

8th Royal Munster Fusiliers

August

Place	Date	Hour	Summary of Events and Information	Remarks and references to Appendices
NOEUX LES MINES.	1/8/16		All Coys paraded Batln at Divisional Baths NOEUX. The Battalion paraded at 11.30 pm to proceed Divis'nt. Cinema, when Parchment Certificates for Gallantry were presented by Lt Col Monteagle-Browne DSO, commanding, to:— Major L. ROCHE, Lieuts F.S. WOODLEY, F.T. BIGGANE, S.K. FURNEY, H.M.V. O'BRIEN. 2nd Lt G.F. MAHER, 2728 R.S.M. E.T. PARROTT, Sup. 6555 MILLER, 187 CROWE, 4854 FITZGIBBON, [REDACTED] Cpl 9198 EYLES, L.Cpl 4103 CUDDIHY, 5201 McMAHON, Pte 3650 DALY, 4290 McGLYNN, 5702 CORBETT, 6057 BLAKE, 3793 BARRETT, 4333 COSTELLOE, 3622 DUNDON, 4246 DOYLE. Certificates were also awarded to 18/190 (killed in action)., 30/7/16 Majr. 2 Lt T. FITZPATRICK (killed in action), 2761 S/L 2/Lt E. HOLLAND (wounded 30.7.16), 221 S/L T. COBB (now in hospital 20.7/16) 2761 S/L T. O'TOOLE (wounded 30.7.16), 3761 Pte. T. MAHONEY (killed in action) Major L. ROCHE rejoined the Battalion 2/Lt. N. HOUGH reported for duty, two posts LG gun. Tenth wire company arrangements for Squad & Arms Drill. Saluting to the Band. Troops dismissed at 6.30 pm.	
	2.8.16			

F. Monteagle-Browne Lieut-Colonel
Comdg 8 (S) Bn R. Munster Fus.

Army Form C. 2118.

WAR DIARY
or
INTELLIGENCE SUMMARY. 5th Royal Hunts Fusiliers

(Erase heading not required.)

Instructions regarding War Diaries and Intelligence Summaries are contained in F.S. Regs., Part II. and the Staff Manual respectively. Title pages will be prepared in manuscript.

Month August

Place	Date	Hour	Summary of Events and Information	Remarks and references to Appendices
NOEUX LES MINES.	3.8.16		Voluntary Service for R.E. at church NOEUX LES MINES at 9 A.M. Corp. Reading Party paraded independently for exercise in ceremonial. Captain E. Scott was detailed for instruction to 44th Infantry Brigade & proceeded to PHILOSOPHE. Lt. H.H. FITZ-GERALD was appointed acting adjutant vice Capt. Scott. The band played at retreat at 6.30 pm.	
	4.8.16		Paraded as yesterday. The inspection of the Battalion by G.O.C. 1st Army which had been ordered for the day was postponed. The band played at retreat at 6.30 pm.	
	5.8.16		Training under coys. arrangements in morning. Selected men from K. Randall parties gave a demonstration of the use of Stevens's Helt Kennard's Rocket & was interesting. Heart letter from G.O.C. 48th Inf Bde. The following message was received by 47th Inf Bde. from G.O.C. 16th Division: "The work done on the PUITS 14 BIS SECTION left after the men of your Brigade has been most excellent. I beg you to convey my appreciation to Capts. CRICHTON & Capt. LLOYD, for all their good work. Sd. W.B. HICKIE Major General, Comd.g 16th (Irish) Division." F.H. Montague Brooke Lieut-Colonel. Comdg. 8th (S) Bn. R. Munster Fus.	

T.134. Wt. W.708-776. 500000. 4/15. Sir J.C. & S.

Army Form C. 2118.

WAR DIARY
or
INTELLIGENCE SUMMARY. 8th Royal Munster Fusiliers

Month: August

(Erase heading not required.)

Instructions regarding War Diaries and Intelligence Summaries are contained in F. S. Regs., Part II. and the Staff Manual respectively. Title pages will be prepared in manuscript.

Place	Date	Hour	Summary of Events and Information	Remarks and references to Appendices
NOEUX LES MINES.	6.8.16		The Battalion paraded for Divine Service (R.E.) at 9 A.M. at Church NOEUX LES MINES. C. of E. paraded 11.15A.M. in Y.M.C.A. Hut. Lieut. S.K. FURNEY & 978 Sergt. N. GIBBONS were detailed as officer + N.C.O. Instructors at 47th Bn. M.G. School at NOEUX. 2/Lt. T.J. O'MEARA & 6 O.R. were detailed as Instructors at 47th Bn. M.G. Schl. NOEUX. 2/Lt. G.F. MAHER was employed as Machine Gun officer during the absence of 2/Lt. FURNEY vice 2/Lt. T.R. COLFER who took over command of the section.	
	7.8.16		The Battalion paraded at Show Ground NOEUX for inspection by G.O.C. 1 Corps at 5 P.M. Also present were G.O.C. 16th Division, G.O.C. 47 INF. BDE. Ribbons newly granted were presented to the following members of the Battalion: 6555 Sgt. MILLER, 4854 Sgt. FITZGIBBON, 2761 Sgt. O'TOOLE, 5407 Sec. Cpl. McMAHON, 4767 Pt. O'SULLIVAN, 772 Pt. HEALY, 3793 Pt. BARRETT, 6057 Pt. BLAKE, 4246 Mc DOYLE. The G.O.C. 1 Corps expressed himself very pleased with the bearing of the men on parade.	

FMcCarthyO'Brien Lieut. Colonel
cmdg. 8th (D) Bn. R. Mun. Fus.

Army Form C. 2118.

WAR DIARY
or
INTELLIGENCE SUMMARY.

(Erase heading not required.)

August — 2w Royal Munster Fusiliers

Place	Date	Hour	Summary of Events and Information	Remarks and references to Appendices
NOEUX LES MINES.	8:8:16		There was a conference for C.O.s, adjutants, 2nd in Command at HQ 47th Inf Bde MAZINGARBE at 10 AM. The Band played & returned at 6.30 pm. The Battalion paraded at 9 pm for night march to outpost scheme, returning to Billets at 4 AM.	
	9.8.16		2/Lt. W.S. WATTS was posted Lieutenant with seniority from 17.12.16. The Battalion moved to billets in MAZINGARBE, S, in Bde Reserve area. The Band played at retreat at 6.30 pm. The following officers reported for duty from leave: Lieut: B.H. GRAY (3rd Leinsters) B Coy 2/Lieut: N.H. UNDERWOOD (3rd Leinsters) A Coy " " H.M.A. OLPHERT (5th Munsters) D Coy " " D.J. KEATING (3rd Munsters) C Coy " " D DE COURCY " " A Coy. " " J. DOYLE " " C Coy.	

FWMontresor Bent Dsr Lieut - Colonel
Comdg. 8th (S) Bn. R munster Fus.

Army Form C. 2118.

WAR DIARY
or
INTELLIGENCE SUMMARY.
(Erase heading not required.)

August   8th Royal Munster Fusiliers

Place	Date	Hour	Summary of Events and Information	Remarks and references to Appendices
MAZING-ARBE.	10.8.16		Training in Bayonet fighting, & bomb throwing under Coy arrangements. The Band played at retreat at 6.30 p.m.	
	11.8.16		All Coys. proceeded to walk at Divis'nt Baths MAZINGARBE. Training during the afternoon in Bayonet fighting under Coy. arrangements. The Band played at retreat at 6.30 p.m.	
	12.8.16		Training under Coy. arrangements. The Commanding Officer held a conference with all officers of the Battalion at H.Q. Mess at 12 noon. Lieut. W.S. WATTS was appointed Assistant Adjt. of the Battalion. The Band Major at retreat at 6.30 p.m. Military Crosses awarded to Lieut S.K. FURNEY & A.H.V. O'BRIEN were pinned by Commanding Officer on parade.	
LEFT SUBSECTION LOOS.	13.8.16		The Battalion relieved the 7th Bn. Leinster Regt. in LEFT SUBSECTION, LOOS. After the relief the disposition of the Coys was as follows:- from left A/B/C/D Coys, B Coy, A Coy in Reserve; C Coy. 2 Lt. DE COURCY proceeded for instruction to Divisn't BOMBING SCH. 2 Lt. DOYLE was attached for duty to B double Regt. S.H.M.V. O'BRIEN with wounded	

F. Montague Bernard
Lieut-Colonel
Comdg. 8th (S) Bn. R. Munn. Fus.

Army Form C. 2118.

WAR DIARY
or
INTELLIGENCE SUMMARY.
(Erase heading not required.)

Army: **8th Royal Munster Fusiliers**
Month: **August**

Place	Date	Hour	Summary of Events and Information	Remarks and references to Appendices
LEFT SUBSECTION LOOS	14.8.16		Usual work of Trench Maintenance was begun. "Thanks" in SUPPORT LINE between BOYAUX 43-44 & main prier between CRASSIER cleared, restored. During afternoon enemy's fallen the CRASSIER with field guns. Our guns retaliated. At 2 A.M. an enemy working party of about 12 men coming from behind SEAFORTH CRATER was dispersed by our Machine Guns. About 3:30 A.M. a loud fire was observed in the enemy line S. of GORDON CRATER. It burned for about 30 minutes. The enemy was heard working with picks in his front line between BOYAU 43 & CAMERON ALLEY. We searched his trench with Mortar Rifle Grenades at the front. At 4:30 A.M. the enemy blew a small mine in the vicinity of SEAFORTH CRATER. Having in a shaft in our front line. There was no cratering, debris from the CRATER. Patrols went out by all coys in the front line.	
	15.8.16		Usual work of Trench Maintenance continued. Work in front line N. of BOYAU 43 thence SCOTS ALLEY deepened. 80' barbed concertina was put up between BOYAUX 40-44. A new O.P. was commenced on the CRASSIER at M 6 G 3/4 6. Enemy Trench Mortars bombarded our Trench on the CRASSIER until silenced by our artillery. Little damage was done to our line. At 1:30 A.M. two Lewis Guns were taken out & heavy Green Moored S. of CAMERON CRATER which had been previously reconnoitered by patrols. Opened fire a range the track of CAMERON &	signed (S) Br. R. Munro, Lieut-Colonel, 8th R.M.F. Friday 8th

Army Form C. 2118.

WAR DIARY
or
INTELLIGENCE SUMMARY.

(Erase heading not required.)

8th Royal Munster Fusiliers

August

Place	Date	Hour	Summary of Events and Information	Remarks and references to Appendices
LEFT SUBSECTION LOOS.	15.8.16		SEAFORTH CRATERS, enfilading the enemy front line for 500x Right Coy. on 1000x in rt. About 12 midnight in retaliation for enemy Trench Mortar activity our Stokes guns from B8/10 41 Avenue on a upper station on railway line running parallel to the CRASSIER in which seven live munroe's were observed. A direct hit were obtained at 2.15 p.m. the enemy put up a small box kite from his front line opposite B9/10 AA. 11 new loops were added later. Then opened fire hostilely attacked M.G.etc. Patrols were sent out by us esp. in front line.	
	16.8.16		Usual work of Trench Maintenance continued. Normal Trench Mortar & Rifle Grenade activity throughout the day. At 1.27 A.M. after 2 minutes intense Trench Mortar preparation a series of raids were carried out on the enemy lines at the SUNKEN ROAD (M.6.c), under Lieut. C. O'H HOUGH. "A" party approached the SAP on E. Up of SUNKEN ROAD under cover of the Hostile Curtain bombed it. After 2 Germans occupying the SAP 2 were killed then wounded. The latter succeeded in making their escape. The party then trailed the enemy Trench to U.Z on the right flank. "B" party under Lt. Howard advanced directly with a R/Lt HOUGH, worked towards the SUNKEN ROAD in to hostile Trench on to left flank. 2nd Lieut. HOWARD made Lieut- Colonel Smedley 8 (A) Bn. R. Munro Fus.	

Army Form C. 2118.

WAR DIARY or INTELLIGENCE SUMMARY.
(Erase heading not required.)

August — 8th Royal Munster Fusiliers

Place	Date	Hour	Summary of Events and Information	Remarks and references to Appendices
LEFT SUBSECTION LOOS	16/8/16		Bombers, Snipers, & probably Infantry came under Machine Gun fire from huge eyes head the enemy were ever fired later when 2 Lt HOUGH fell wounded. He had 2 men been wounded. The Machine Gun which opened fire on the party was brought into a dugout hurriedly on hearing of Captain me & brought his action to the principal front rank man found on "C" party which had been ordered to reinforce us in case we were cut off on hospital party "C" party, which had been ordered to reinforce us in case we were cut in the we & caused most did not come into action. D party, when operation started the SAP which was held by the enemy at the time effected his SAP near the CRASSIER forced the 1st & done offensive. The strength of the party down the but were unable to cross it any 10th gave that A/party the command of the SAP SUNKEN ROAD was effected without loss. 2 ( ) Lt HOUGH & 9 Lt 20 OR. shots took part in attempts dominating the Loss. 2 additional Lt HOUGH & 9 Lt 20 OR. shots took part in attempts 3 were killed 82 wounded. The loss of the enemy must have been considerable from OS Lts command @5pm the Left Guards entered myself Rata. by trenches known @ Bondy M. even Sub Main Trench which we held in four by force @ ( ) Bond & Kelly — We will the Road trenches. The enemy retaliated heavily with artillery & heavy mortars — but did no damage to our trenches.	

F. M. Stapelford Bindle Lieut. Colonel
Cmdg. 8th (S) Bn. R. Munster. Fus.

Army Form C. 2118.

WAR DIARY
or
INTELLIGENCE SUMMARY.   8th Royal Munster Fusiliers
(Erase heading not required.)

Place	Date	Hour	Summary of Events and Information	Remarks and references to Appendices
LEFT SUBSECTION LOOS	17.8.16		Work of Trench Maintenance continued. Enemy artillery Trench Mortars were unpetive in early morning in vicinity of CRASSIER until silenced by our artillery & rifle Grens. The Battalion was relieved by 7th Bn. Seaforth Regt. & moved to K.R.A. Support lines when the Coys were disposed as follows: VILLAGE LINE B Coy. DUKE STREET, D Coy. ENCLOSURE A & C Coys.	
BDE. SUPPORT LOOS	18.8.16		Work of Trench Maintenance begun in VILLAGE LINE TENS ROAD REDOUBT. 2 Lys. parties of 66 OR. were found to 173 Tunnelling Coy. R.E. + 1/63 OR for 258 Tunnelling Coy. R.E. Our field artillery was intermittently active throughout the day. 2 Lt. Alfred Underwood Keating was attached for duty by Irish Rif. 2 Lt. Bishop ARNOLD & BROWN of 7th Irish Regt. was attached to the Battalion for duty. Postas & Plans: 2 Lt. BISHOP C Coy. 2 Lts. ARNOLD & BROWN D Coy.	
LOOS	19.8.16		Work of Trench Maintenance Continued. In addition 2 Rifle parties found yesterday, carrying parties of 58 OR for Both R.E., Stores &OS were obtained for the Battalion. Enemy heavy Trench Mortar was very active on left Subsection from about 5 pm. Our artillery & Stokes Mortars replied.	

Illegible signature Lieut-Colonel
Comdg. 8th (S) Bn. R. Muns. Fus.

T2134. Wt. W708—776. 500000. 4/15. Sir J. C. & S.

Army Form C. 2118.

WAR DIARY
or
INTELLIGENCE SUMMARY.
(Erase heading not required.)

8th Royal Munster Fusiliers

Place	Date	Hour	Summary of Events and Information	Remarks and references to Appendices
BDE. SUPPORT. LOOS	20.8.16		Work of Trench Maintenance continued. Working parts as yesterday. Saw the parts detailed for work with 173 Tunnelling Coy R.E. were cancelled because from Estaples we received out by 5 Royal Muns. Rof. The Battalion relieved the 24th Seaforth Rgt. in Left Subsector LOOS. after about the disposition was as follows from Left B Right: D Coy., B Coy., C Coy., In Reserve A Coy at 4.15 pm	
LEFT SUBSECTION LOOS	21.8.16		on Stokes trench mortars were active, the enemy replying industriously with aerial Torpedos. At 4.35 pm. we sent a Camouflets of SEAFORTH CRATER. During the night we established NO MANS LAND by a system of bombing posts on the CRATERS & the GREEN MOUND with covering parties lodging the time in front & following onto form reentrants craters as our own wire, each reentrant angle being closed by a Lewis Machine Gun. No attempt was made to approach our lines during the night. Patrols were sent out by Coys. in front line	
	22.8.16		Work of Trench Maintenance continued. A block in trench line between BOXROX 43–44 30 × 6 was cleared. 30 × were erected on Centre Coy Front. In retaliation for enemy Trench Mortar activity on French Mortars bombarded the enemy lines. Without Support without special between BOXROX 41–43. The enemy Mortar Artillery and Wind Torpedoes replied, will Infantino weight Gratel & Ornamentation. This enemy however was poor. During the night we encountered NO MANS	

Ed Mc Reynolds 2nd Capt
Cmdg 8th (S) Bn. R. Munster Fus.
Lieut - Colonel

Army Form C. 2118.

WAR DIARY
or
INTELLIGENCE SUMMARY.

(Erase heading not required.)

8th Royal Munster Fusilier

Place	Date	Hour	Summary of Events and Information	Remarks and references to Appendices
LEFT SUBSECTION LOOS.	22.8.16		LAND by the Scout dispatches were employed last night. The enemy appeared uneasy & harassed by our wire on our front repeatedly during the night. A working party was located by our patrol on the SUNKEN ROAD & dispersed by Machine Gun fire. Capt. WATTS-RUS- SELL proceeded on leave to England.	
	23.8.16		Work of Trench maintenance continued. Damaged trench between BOYAUX 43 & 44 for support. A good deal of talking was heard in enemy line on our front. At one point the enemy called out to our men "You can have them trenches till we are on the 27th". We replied with Salvos of rifle grenades. About 4.30 p.m. the enemy Trench Mortars were fairly active until silenced by our artillery & Stokes Guns. During the night we established No MANS LAND on our two previous nights. Patrols were sent out by all coys in front line	
	24.8.16		The Battalion was relieved by the 12th Bn South Wales Borderers & proceeded to Billets at LES BREBIS. Capts CRICHTON & CAIRN DUFF rejoined the Battalion for duty & were posted to D & C coys respectively. Casualties during tour of Trenches 13-24.8.16 Killed 5 O.R. Wounded. 2t H.M.V. O'BRIEN, 2Lt. W. HOUGH, & 34 O.R. Wounded (at Duty) Major L. ROCHE	

F. W. Montagu Moore
Lieut. Colonel
Comdg. 8th (S Bn. Royal Munster Fus.

Army Form C. 2118.

WAR DIARY
or
INTELLIGENCE SUMMARY.
(Erase heading not required.)

8th Royal Munster Fusiliers

Place	Date	Hour	Summary of Events and Information	Remarks and references to Appendices
LES BREBIS	25.6.16		The following drafts arrived for the Battalion from (late) Coy: 44 OR from 11th Entrenching Battalion. 83 OR from 16th Infantry Base Depot Etaples. The Battalion paraded at 11.15 & moved to MARLE-LES-MINES via NOEUX & BRUAY to Billets, arriving at 6.30 pm	
MARLE-LES-MINES	26.6.16		The Battalion paraded at 10 AM & moved to BURBURE via LOZINGHEM & ALLOUAGNE to Billets arriving at 6.30 pm.	
BURBURE	27.6.16		The Battalion received orders to entrain at CHOCQUES on night of 28/29th for LONGEAU. All coys. paraded for clothing at Quartermaster Stores. Baths were arranged by Coys. for the men. The Coys. paraded independently at 8 AM for Divine Service at Church BURBURE. Capt T.C. CAIRN DUFF was appointed for Instruction in Bombing. The band played at retreat at 6.30 pm	
	28.8.16		The Battalion received orders changing place of entrainment from LONGEAU to HEILLY. The band played at retreat at 6.30 pm.	

FMFitzgerald Lieut-Colonel
Comdg. 8th (S) Bn. R. Munro Fus.

Army Form C. 2118.

WAR DIARY
or
INTELLIGENCE SUMMARY.
(Erase heading not required.)

August   8th Royal Munster Fusiliers

Place	Date	Hour	Summary of Events and Information	Remarks and references to Appendices
BURBURE	29.8.16		The Battalion moved at 6.30 AM to CHOCQUES, entrained travelling by ST. POL FLIXCOURT & AMIENS to HEILLY, where it arrived at 8.40 pm. Proceeded to the SAND PIT S of MÉAULTE to Bivouac.	
SAND PIT	30.8.16		Weather continuously wet. Order received to proceed on following day to CITADEL CAMP on FRICOURT ROAD.	
CITADEL CAMP— GUILLEMONT	31.8.16	10.20 AM 1.20 pm	The Battalion moved at 10.20 AM to CITADEL CAMP where it arrived at 1.20 pm. Order received that 167th Brigade would relieve the 60th Brigade between GUILLEMONT & WATERLOT FARM. The Battalion moved at 5pm to Bde. Support line in BERNAFAY WOOD when it relieved the 12th Bn. Kings Royal Rifle Corps. BERNAFAY WOOD was subjected by the enemy to an intense bombardment with lachrymatory shells.	

G.M. Stephenson
Lieut-Colonel
Comdg. 8th (S) Bn. R. Mund. Fus.

47/6

WAR DIARY.

8th Royal Munster Fusiliers

MONTH OF September 1916.

VOLUME:-

Army Form C. 2118.

WAR DIARY
or
INTELLIGENCE SUMMARY.   8th Royal Munster Fusiliers
Month: September
(Erase heading not required.)

Instructions regarding War Diaries and Intelligence Summaries are contained in F.S. Regs., Part II. and the Staff Manual respectively. Title pages will be prepared in manuscript.

Place	Date	Hour	Summary of Events and Information	Remarks and references to Appendices
BARNAFAY WOOD	1.9.16		Our artillery of all calibre continuously active during the day. After dark the enemy bombarded our positions heavily with Gas + Lachrymatory shells. The following officers of the Bn. were evacuated suffering from the effects of Gas poisoning. Capt. J.C. CAIRN DUFF, 2/Lt. T. O'MEARA + F. BISHOP. Gassed (at duty) Lt. Colonel E. MONTEAGLE-BROWNE D.S.O. L/f.	
	2.9.16		Continuance of artillery activity. Orders received that the Battalion will take part in the attack on the German positions at GUILLEMONT on the following day. Conference of officers at 11 AM. The G.O.C. 16th Div. visited the battalion. After dark the enemy again shelled our positions in BARNAFAY WOOD with gas Shells. W/f.	
GUILLEMONT	3.9.16		The Battalion moved into position in the "GRIDIRON" at 3 AM. The companies were disposed as follows:- R. front A coy under Major L. ROCHE + Capt. J.H. LAWLOR. Left front B coy under Major T.A.N. BOLTON & Lieut. WOODLEY. In command of front line Major T.J. O'BRIEN. In support of A coy. C coy under Capt. C.W. CHANDLER + 2/Lt. F. ARNOLD. In support of B coy. D coy. under Capt. R.H. CRICHTON + 2/Lt. F. BROWN. In command of support Coy. Major W. McC. CROSBIE. In command of Machine Gun Section Lieut. F.K. FURNEY and Lieut J.R. COLFER	

J. O'Brien Major
Commdg. 8th R.M.F.

Army Form C. 2118.

WAR DIARY
or
INTELLIGENCE SUMMARY.   8th Royal Munster Fusiliers
(Erase heading not required.)

Month: September

Place	Date	Hour	Summary of Events and Information	Remarks and references to Appendices
GUILLEMONT	9.9.16		The leading companies left their trench together with 6th CONNAUGHTS. At 12.30 pm the enemy had been cleared from GUILLEMONT the QUARRIES, & Battalion HQ establd in the village. At 2.35 pm. when the artillery barrage had lifted the Battalion advanced to the SUNKEN ROAD E of GUILLEMONT when it established itself at 2.45pm. Consolidated Reported. The failure of the 16th on left flank (not its advance on GINCHY) exposed the left flank of the Battalion to danger of being turned. Three heavy counts which preceded by artillery preparation were repulsed. The Battalion was relieved at 2 AM at SUNKEN ROAD by 12th KINGS ROYAL RIFLES & proceeded to Road N.1	
	10.9.16		BARNAFAY WOOD. The chaplain Capt the Rev J.WRAFTER S.J. accompanied the Battalion during the operation. Casualties: 265 all ranks. The following officers were wounded: Major T.J. O'BRIEN (at duty), Major W.Mc.C.CROSBIE, Capt C.W.CHANDLER R.H.CRICHTON, J.H.LAWLOR, Lieuts: F.WOODLEY (at duty) S.WATTS (died of wounds). 2 Lieut M.J. SHEEHAN (Shell Shock), Lt. CHEESEMAN (R.A.M.C). Headquarters Staff present at the Engagement were: Lieut. Colonel E. MONTEAGLE-BROWNE D.S.O. Commanding. Major T.J.O'BRIEN 2 i/c, Lieut H.H.FITZ-GERALD adjutant, Lieut S.WATTS asst. adjutant. Lieut H.D. CREGAN Signalling officer. J.J.O'Brien Major Comdg 8th R.M.F	

Army Form C. 2118.

WAR DIARY
or
INTELLIGENCE SUMMARY.
(Erase heading not required.)

8th Royal Munster Fusiliers

Title pages September

Place	Date	Hour	Summary of Events and Information	Remarks and references to Appendices
BARNAFAY WOOD	4/9/16		The Battalion proceeded at 8.30 p.m. to Camp at CARNOY. Capt WATTS-RUSSELL returned from leave. 2/Lieut C.L. SWEENEY & G. DONNELLY joined the Battalion. Capt BLACK R.A.M.C. was attached for Battalion in 2/Lt CHEESMAN. R.A.M.C. (wounded) Major T.A.N. BOLTON went Hospital sick	
CARNOY	5.9.16		The Battalion was employed cleaning up refitting. Lieut S.K. FURNEY went to hospital sick	
	6.9.16		Coys paraded for inspections of kit & equipment. The adjutant attended a conference at Bde. H.Q. sick	
GINCHY	7.9.16		Major O'BRIEN attended a conference for C.O.s at Bde H.Q. vice C.O. (sick). The Battalion received orders to leave Wh SUNKEN ROAD E of GUILLEMONT. Lieut of duty 2/Lt E. KEANE joined the DUBLINS at 12 midnight, under command Major O'BRIEN. The Coys were disposed as follows: left front C coy under 2/Lt F. ARNOLD & E.T. KEANE. Right front D coy under Capt T. WATTS-RUSSELL & 2/Lt F.B. BROWN. Left Support A coy under 2/Lt C.L. SWEENEY. Right Support B coy under	

Comdg 8 R.M.F.

Army Form C. 2118.

WAR DIARY
or
INTELLIGENCE SUMMARY.

(Erase heading not required.)

8th Royal Munster Fusiliers September

Instructions regarding War Diaries and Intelligence Summaries are contained in F.S. Regs., Part II. and the Staff Manual respectively. Title pages will be prepared in manuscript.

Place	Date	Hour	Summary of Events and Information	Remarks and references to Appendices
GINCHY	7.9.16		Lieut F. WOODLEY M	
	8.9.16		Continuous activity of our artillery. The enemy Snipers M	
	9.9.16		Lieut Col. E. MONTEAGLE-BROWNE took over command of the Battalion. There was a conference of officers at Bn. HQ at 10 AM at 4.40 pm the Battalion left the trenches on SUNKEN ROAD to attack Enemy line. On their arrival at the front had been lashed by our artillery fire with Mg [illegible] men & machine guns it was impossible to carry it by a frontal attack [illegible] The leading company of the Battalion however penetrated into the position. The Battalion was relieved at 3.30 AM by 3rd Grenadier Guards. Casualties 76 OR. 4th Major A.H. Murray Officers Killed 2 Lieut. F. BROWN. Wounded Capt. T. WATTS-RUSSELL, 2 Lieuts. F. ARNOLD, C.L. SWEENEY, E.J. KEANE M	
BRICKFIELDS	10.9.16		The Battalion proceeded to the BRICKFIELDS arriving at 6.30 AM. The Battalion fell in at 2 pm. Proceeded to the HAPPY VALLY when it bivouacked. 2 Lts. D.A. BUTLER [illegible], H.B. FISHER & J.P. MURROUGH joined the Battalion. [illegible] took over Command 4(A.C.D. Coys [illegible])	

Army Form C. 2118.

WAR DIARY
or
INTELLIGENCE SUMMARY.   8th Royal Munster Fusiliers

(Erase heading not required.)

Instructions regarding War Diaries and Intelligence Summaries are contained in F. S. Regs., Part II. and the Staff Manual respectively. Title pages will be prepared in manuscript.

Place	Date	Hour	Summary of Events and Information	Remarks and references to Appendices
VAUX-S-SOMME	11.9.16		The Battalion moved at 4 pm to VILLE-sur-SOMME, where it arrived at 6.30 pm. Major T.A.N. BOLTON reported for duty. W/	
	12.9.16		The Battalion found working parties for preparation of a Rifle Range (Bombing). Found The First Major also returned at 6.30 pm. W/	
	13.9.16		Training commenced in Musketry under 2/Lt FISHER. Bombing under Sgt. FITZGIBBON, close order Drill, Manual of Arms, Saluting. W/	
	14.9.16		Training continued. 2/Lt J.F. GLEESON reported the Battalion. Park are command of A Coy. 2/Lt F. WOODLEY was transferred to C coy. Took over command of B Coy. W/	
	15.9.16		Training continued. A concert was held under Brigade arrangements at the Chateau VAUX. W/	

Morrison Major
Commdg 8th R.M.F.

Army Form C. 2118.

WAR DIARY
or
INTELLIGENCE SUMMARY.
(Erase heading not required.)

September   1st Royal Munster Fusiliers

Place	Date	Hour	Summary of Events and Information	Remarks and references to Appendices
VAUX S. SOMME	16/9/16		Training Continued. Sports were held under Brigade Arrangements at VAUX commencing at 2 pm, in which the Battalion won the following events: Tug of War, 440, Staff ride, & Second 2nd Place in Wrestling on horseback.	
	17/9/16		The Transport, Machine Gun Section, & Trench Mortar Personnel moved to new Billets area at HUPPY via LONGPRÉ.	
HUCHENNEVILLE	18/9/16		The Battalion fell in at 10 AM & marched to CORBIE from where it proceeded by train via AMIENS – LONGPRÉ to Billets in HUCHENNEVILLE. 7 Corps was billetted in billets: at HUCHENNEVILLE Headquarters, C Coy, Machine Gun Section, Transport; at VILLERS, A, B, D. Coy's. w.h.	
	19/9/16		Check parade was held by all Coys. 2/Lt. G.F. MAHER returned from leave. Major over command of A Coy. w.h.	

J.J. Parrin Major
Comdg 1st R.M.F.

Army Form C. 2118.

WAR DIARY
or
INTELLIGENCE SUMMARY.
(Erase heading not required.)

Month: September
8th Royal Munster Fusiliers

Place	Date	Hour	Summary of Events and Information	Remarks and references to Appendices
HUCHENNEVILLE	20.9.16		A party of 16 O.R. left for instruction in Lewis Machine Guns at ÉTAPLES, a billeting party under command of 2/Lt BUTLER left at midnight for ABBEVILLE to reconnoitre new billeting area. M.F.	
	21.9.16		The Battalion marched to ABBEVILLE where it entrained, proceeding to BAILLEUL via CALAIS & HAZEBROUCK, where it moved to billets at METEREN. M.F.	
METEREN	22.9.16		The Battalion arrived at METEREN at 3.30 am. The G.O.C. 47th Inf. Bde. inspected the billets of the Battalion. A reinforcing draft of 30 OR arrived for the Battalion. The Band played at retreat at 6.30 pm. M.F.	
	23.9.16		2/Lts M. NUNAN, F.W. MOLONY, & W. MOLONY joined the Battalion, and were posted to C M.G Coys respectively. During the afternoon inter company football matches were played off. Lieut. M.D. CREGAN proceeded on 10 days leave to Ireland. Battalion under command of 2/Lt H.D. BUTLER. M.F.	

Morris Magee
Comdg 8th R.M.F.

Army Form C. 2118.

WAR DIARY
or
INTELLIGENCE SUMMARY.

(Erase heading not required.)

8th Royal Munster Fusiliers

Title pages September

Place	Date	Hour	Summary of Events and Information	Remarks and references to Appendices
LOCRE	24.9.16		Coys. paraded independently for Divine Service in Church METEREN at 7 pm. The Battalion marched to LOCRE line ST. JEAN CAPEL where it was inspected by G.O.C. 47th Div. Bde. Ist March. The Battalion arrived at 12 noon and was billeted in Huts. O.C. Coys. went up to reconnoitre the line, Right Section. W.F.	
	25.9.16		The Battalion paraded at 11.15 AM together with 6th Connaught Rangers [?] inspection by G.O.C. 2nd Army. The Coys. paraded for Baths during the afternoon. W.F.	
	26.9.16		O.C. Coys. M.G.O., 2 i/c, & Adjt. reconnoitred line Left Section. Coys. paraded for Bayonet fighting, Gas helmet & Close order Drill, Bombing. W.F.	
B.DE. SUPPORT LINE [SIEGE FARM]	27.9.16		All Coys. paraded for Walk from 9 AM. The Battalion marched off at 2:30 pm to take over to yard Support positions. The disposition of the Coys. were as follows. 2 KIMMEL VILLAGE. A & B Coys. at SIEGE FARM. C & D Coys. Headquarters at Colonel E. MONTEAGLE-BROWNE D.S.O. having proceeded on leave to England. Major T.J. O'BRIEN took over command of the Battalion. W.F.	

M. O'Brien Major
Commdg. 8th R.M.F.

Army Form C. 2118.

WAR DIARY
or
INTELLIGENCE SUMMARY.
(Erase heading not required.)

8th Royal Munster Fusiliers

September

Place	Date	Hour	Summary of Events and Information	Remarks and references to Appendices
BDE SUPPORT [SIEGE FARM]	28.9.16		Coys. practised in training in Bayonet fighting, Physical Drill, Sanitary Squad & Musketry drill. C.Coy 5th M.G.C. accommodated at farm. The following officers joined the Battalion. 2Lt E.E. FORAN, J. REIDY, J.F. FULLEN, 2Lt J. ROBINSON went on leave to Ireland. M/L	
	29.9.16		Training Continued. A reinforcement draft of 15 OR joined the Battalion. M/L	
	30.9.16		Training Continued. NCOs & OR from Battalion were attached to the pioneers. R.S.M. E.J. PARROTT was promoted to the rank of Lieutenant. A siren guard was turned out by the Bde on an Lt at 10 pm after seven artillery preparation. M/L	

M. O'Brien Major
Comdg 8th R.M.F.
1-10-16

WAR DIARY

MONTH OF OCTOBER, 1916.

VOLUME 11

8th Royal Munster Fusiliers

WAR DIARY or INTELLIGENCE SUMMARY

Army Form C. 2118

(Erase heading not required.)

8th Royal Munster Fusiliers

654d

Place	Date	Hour	Summary of Events and Information	Remarks and references to Appendices
LEFT SECTION 16th DIV- AREA (N.18.a - N.24.a)	1.10.16		The Battalion relieved the 6th Connaught Rangers in Left Section, 16th Divisional Area. After relief the Coys. were disposed as follows: Left B Coy. Centre D Coy. Right C Coy. In Support A Coy. Bn. HQ at YORK HOUSE. Sc. FRONT LINE: Capt. T.A.N. BOLTON. Patrols were sent out by Coys. in their own line. All available men were employed (a) nightly sending rations and at Advanced posts of the trench (b) erecting a strong traverse at the junction of WATLING STREET & the Advanced Line (c) Draining. The line in this section (used & exposed to enemy observation & Sniping. Enemy activity was confined to Mr of Machine Gun & Trench Mortar Bursts fired to which we retaliated. 2 Lieuts. E.P. HARTIGAN, & J.E. WALSH joined the Battalion for duty. Were posted to A & C Coys. respectively.	
	2.10.16		Repairs of trenches continued. 30" of parapet which had fallen in every to rain & opposite K.I.N. was cleared & sand bags filled & stacked ready to be placed in position after dark. Enemy Sniper active during the day, at night an Officers patrol went out from Wedge/h garden and worked N. through K.18.2. Sounds of distinct stakes were heard from the enemy front line. On the return of this our Stokes guns fired on the part of the line. Two enemy Machine Guns were in action in the Reserve Line in front of PETIT BOIS. An enemy searchlight was observed repeatedly on our fly & Coy Front, & it appeared to be mounted on a mounted car.	
	3.10.16		Repairs of trenches continued. The parapet had to be pulled down further at the following points. K.I.N., N.18.1., N.18.2., N.24.10. At K.I. where an live mine & a sharp edge overhead "wire" cover was erected. At 1.15 pm the enemy burst 12 light shrapnel shells over our left half of his line. A salvo of heavy trench Morter Bombs were sent into 16 enemy trenches in the vicinity of WATLING STREET. An artillery retaliation shortly on both occasions. A patrol went out from our line at Junction of WARK LANE & the enemy front line, along the enemy were. No hostile patrols were encountered. Sounds of digging were heard in the enemy front line, which the Stokes guns subsequently at the point. 2 O.R. rejoined on draft	

E. M. Westropp
Major
Comdy 8th Munster Fusrs.

WAR DIARY or INTELLIGENCE SUMMARY

Army Form C. 2118

October — 8th Royal Munster Fusiliers

Place	Date	Hour	Summary of Events and Information	Remarks and references to Appendices
LEFT SECTION 16th DIVL AREA (N.18.a – N.24.a)	4.10.16		Repair of trenches continued. A tramway with wich shelter commenced between N.18.2 – N.18.3. South end between K.1.N & N.24.10. Deepened Enemy Sniper active. Some aerial torpedoes were sent from enemy support line against our Right. Machine Gun position but fell short. An enemy patrol was caught by our machine gun but it is not thought our left coy about this period. Snipers were heard. Our patrols reported that no work was in progress in the enemy trenches.	
BDE RESERVE. BUTTERFLY FARM (M.19.a.7.10)	5.10.16		Repair of trenches continued. Three screens were erected at most exposed parks of R[ight] coy front. Enemy Sniping activity continued. 8th Battalion relieved by 7th Leinsters 12(?) Proceeded to Camp at BUTTERFLY FARM M.19.a.7.10. arriving at 11 pm. Casualties during tour of the trenches 1-5/10/16 : Killed 1 OR Wounded 4 OR	
	6.10.16		The Battalion was employed cleaning up equipment, the day drawn found the tents – the lining in a very wet condition. Two cook shelters were blown off each half Battalion. Trench Guards were laid down throughout the camp. The Reveil played at Retreat at 6.30 p.m.	
	7.10.16		Young officers formed for instruction is salutary under the Regimental Sergeant Major. The Commander placed inspected the Lewis & C. B. Coys & the Machine Gun Section at 11 am. The inspection was followed by foot inspection. The M.O. 7th Battalion paraded at 3 pm in Camp when the G.O.C. 47th Infantry Brigade presented 16th Divisional Purchases Certificate to the Mess Officer then. Major J.J. O'BRIEN Capt. & Rev. T. WRAFTER S.J. C.F. Lieut. (casy). M.H. FITZ-GERALD. Lieut. F.S. WOODLEY. Lieut. J. COLFER. O.W.E. PARROTT	

signed Lieut. Colonel Comdg. 8th Rl Mund. Fus.

1875 Wt. W593/826 1,000,000 4/15 J.B.C. & A. A.D.S.S./Forms/C. 2118.

WAR DIARY or INTELLIGENCE SUMMARY

Army Form C. 2118

8th Royal Munster Fusiliers

October

Place	Date	Hour	Summary of Events and Information	Remarks and references to Appendices
BDE. RESERVE BUTTER-FLY FARM (M.19.a.7.10)	7.10.16		No 1/5994. R.S.M. T. LEWIS, 3813 Sec.Cpl. T BRENNAN, 2739 Sgt. W. WATSON, 4299 La. Cpl. T. PHILBIN, 3263 Pte. S. LEHANE, 471 Sgt. C. HANRAHAN.	
	8.10.16		Young officer paraded at 9 a.m. under R.S.M & instruction in Saluting. Coy. paraded for Divine Service (R.C) at BUTTERFLY FARM at 6 AM. at 3 pm a series of inter company contests in Tug of War were held & the final at 4 pm. The G.O.C. 16th Division was present. The following Awards Recently made known by wire from G.O.C. 16th Division: Military Cross :- Capt. W. Rev. JOSEPH WRAFFER S.J. C.F., Lieut. FABIAN WOODLEY, Lieut. FREDERICK ARNOLD. Distinguished Conduct Medal 1/5994 R.S.M. JOHN LEWIS. Capt. W. Rev. T. WRAFFER [illegible] & 2nd Lieut. Quartermaster J. REGAN [illegible] on leave. 2nd Lieut E. PARROTT took over the duties of a/Quartermaster.	
	9.10.16		Training as follows; Wiring under 2/Lt. HARRIGAN, Bombing under Sgt. FITZGIBBON, Bayonet fighting & Physical Training under Lieut. GLEESON, destruction session in Rapid adjustment of Box Respirators, Close order Drill. The G.O.C. 8 Infantry Brigade interviewed all officers who had recently joined as orderly Room.	

F.W. FitzGibbon

Lieut Colonel

Comdg. 8/Rl Munst Fus's.

Army Form C. 2118

WAR DIARY or INTELLIGENCE SUMMARY

(Erase heading not required.)

8th Royal Munster Fusiliers   October

Place	Date	Hour	Summary of Events and Information	Remarks and references to Appendices
BDE. RESERVE BUTTERFLY FARM. (M.19.a.7.10)	10.10.16		Battalion proceeded to Baths at LOCRE. The C.O. inspected the line in the afternoon. Coy. Officers + 50% of N.C.O.s of each Coy. reconnoitered the inland route to the line. The Transport Officer reported off leave.	
	11.10.16		Training as follows: Bombing under Sergt. FITZGIBBON, Bayonet fighting Physical Drill under 2/Lt. GLEESON. Snipers on Range. Close order Drill. A Drying Room was begun at BUTTERFLY FARM. Machine Gun Section which was on fatigue on previous day proceeded to Baths at LOCRE. Captn. A.B. BATEMAN R.A.M.C. joined the Battalion for duty vice Capt. E.H. BLACK R.A.M.C. attached to 77th Bde R.F.A. A reinforcing draft of 17 O.R. joined the Battalion.	657d
	12.10.16		Training as follows: Bombing under Sergt. FITZGIBBON, Bayonet fighting & Physical Drill under 2/Lt. GLEESON. Machine Gun Section on Range. Close order Drill. Instruction & exercise in Rapid Adjustment of Box Respirator.	

J. W. Montagu Hyde DSO
Lieut. Colonel
Comdg. 8th Bn. Royal Munster Fusrs.

Army Form C. 2118

WAR DIARY or INTELLIGENCE SUMMARY

8th Royal Munster Fusiliers

October

Place	Date	Hour	Summary of Events and Information	Remarks and references to Appendices
BOE. SUPPORT. SIEGE FARM. (N.16.c.2.7)	13.10.16		The Battalion relieved the 7th Leinster Regt. in BOE. SUPPORT Billets. Afterwards the disposition of the Coys. was as follows:- H.Q. & A & B Coys. at SIEGE FARM. (N.16.c.2.7) C & D Coys at KIMMEL. Capt. T.A.N. BOLTON proceeded to England to attend a course of instruction at Aldershot. 2nd Lt. J.T. REIDY took over command of B Coy. The following Immediate Rewards were notified by wire from G.O.C. 1st Division:- Distinguished Service Order - Major W.McC. CROSBIE. Military Cross - Capt. C. W. CHANDLER. The Band played Retreat at 6.30 p.m. at SIEGE FARM. 2 O.R. proceeded on leave.	
	14.10.16		Inspection of Box Respirators of all coys by M.O. O.C. all coys, H.G.O. + T.M.O. reconnoitred the positions to be taken up by the Battalion in case of attack. The Band played at Retreat at 6.30 p.m.	
	15.10.16		D.A.A. & Q.M.G. 16th Division with Staff Captain 47th Infantry Bde. inspected the kits of officers who had been recommended to proceed to France for Temp. Captain while in command of a Company. All officers & 50% of N.C.Os of each coy. reconnoitred Battalions Battle positions. Draft of 9 O.R. joined the Battalion. Lieut. Colonel E. MONTEAGLE-BROWNE D.S.O. returned from leave.	658

F.Monteagle-Browne
Lieut. Colonel
Comdg. 8th R.L. Munster Fus.

WAR DIARY
or
INTELLIGENCE SUMMARY

Army Form C. 2118

(Erase heading not required.)

October — 8th Royal Munster Fusiliers

Place	Date	Hour	Summary of Events and Information	Remarks and references to Appendices
BDE. SUPPORT. SIEGE FARM — (N.16.C.2.7)	16/10/16		Test Gas attack at 12.40 p.m. Lieut WOODLEY & 2nd Lieut GLEESON posted. 2nd Lieut WOODLEY & Temp Capt. WILD in command of Coys. WD lifted from 4.10.16, & 13.10.16. refer WW	
LEFT SECTION.	17/10/16		The C.O. held a Conference of officers at Bn. H.Q. at 10. A.M. The Battalion relieved the 6th Connaught Rangers in Left Section 16th Divisional Area after relief the disposition of the Coys was as follows: Left A Coy Centre B Coy Right D Coy. J. Sullivan C Coy — 1 platoon (in SAND BAG VILLA). Headquarters at YORK HOUSE. 4854 Sgt. G. FITZGIBBON proceeded to Infantry Cadet School at BLENDECQUES. J. BUTLER W/posed from hospital & took over command of B Coy. Major J O'BRIEN & 2nd Lt E. PARROTT McGrath on leave to Sullivan Takes Send Party all coys in the line reported that the Sound of work were heard in Enemy front line. Snipers were active on both sides during the night. A search light located at BRICKSTACK at O.19.a.6.2.10 Sweeps our lines repeatedly. NO MAN'S LAND.	65/W
16th DIVL AREA. —	18.10.16		Tuesday restored when the hat Gallipoli at various points along left Coy front amounted to about 15 in all. Enemy S.S. shortened a Centre Coy front on reaching of N.18.1. During the day we were relieved with Rifle Grenades & Stokes Guns. Our artillery were in action at 7.30 p.m. & 10 p.m. There was no retaliation from 7.30 p.m. Montague Mote Lieut Colonel Comdg 8/RMF and Bn. Lieut Colonel	

Army Form C. 2118

WAR DIARY or INTELLIGENCE SUMMARY

8th Royal Munster Fusiliers

October

660d

Place	Date	Hour	Summary of Events and Information	Remarks and references to Appendices
LEFT SECTION 16th DIVL. AREA	18/10/16		An enemy search light was exposed at intervals from N.18.b.1. An each occasion our machine guns opened on this spot. The searchlight was eventually put out of action. Our Machine Gun Claims to have dispersed a party of the enemy working at N.18.5. Third Section and by coy. in the line report that no work was in progress in the Enemy front line. Lt. J. CREGAN returned from leave.	
	19.10.16		The parapet Collapsed at Map. 62, 54, 58, 59 & over 28' in all. C/oy 3rd S. J.N.151. All available men were employed rebuilding the gaps + also on drainage of Trench between Map 39-43. Enemy artillery were active against the enemy portion in rear of our front line system. There was no retaliation. During the day enemy mortars were active on right ½ of D Section – no shells falling however within our front. At night our Machine Guns tested + silenced an enemy gun near N.18.d.5.6. Patrols were sent out by all coys in the line. Lieut. Quartermaster J. REGAN returned from leave. At 2 am	
	20.10.16		Repair of trench continued. Trench boards raised + trench drained between Map 72-74. At Map 72 parapet restored where it had collapsed. During the day several of our aeroplanes reconnoitred the enemy line on our front from a low altitude, probably truth Halkin Gun. All line wire cut patrols were sent out by all coys in the line. A small wiring party was located opposite May 71 dispersed upon Lewis Gun. Sniper were active on both sides during the night. 1 OR proceeded on leave. 2 Lt. HARTIGAN & 2 OR proceeded on a course of instruction in Sniping to 2nd Army School at TERDEGHEM.	

F W Hartigan Lt   Lieut Colonel
Cmdg 8th Munr Fus

WAR DIARY or INTELLIGENCE SUMMARY

Army Form C. 2118

October — 8th Royal Munster Fusiliers

Place	Date	Hour	Summary of Events and Information	Remarks and references to Appendices
LEFT SECTION 16th DIVL AREA	21.10.16		Repair of Trenches Continued. We were active throughout the day with Stokes Guns (Rifle Grenade) Our Snipers were continuously in action against some two with Trench Mortar UNNAMED WOOD. The Battalion was relieved by the 9th Irish Regt. Proceeded to Camp at LA CLYTTE (M.6.d), arriving at 9.30 pm	
DIV. RESERVE LA CLYTTE (M.6.d)	22.10.16		Battalion employed Cleaning Kits Equipment. Ten Permit Condition of the Camp. Camp handed independently by Divine Service (R.E.) at Church LA CLYTTE at 8.15 am. The Band played at Retreat at 6.30 pm	
	23.10.16		The Battalion proceeded to Kirk at WESTOUTRE from 8 am – 12 noon. 2 Lieut NUNAN & 4 OR proceeded to Course of Instruction in Physical Training at M.4.c.4.2. 2 Lt. DONNELLY & 10 OR proceeded on Course of Trench Mortar Work at TERDEGHEM. 2 Lt MURROGH & 16 R Bombing. Training: Bombing, Bayonet Fighting, Physical & Close Order Drill, Machine Gun Section on Range	

F.W.I.Y.Blake
Lieut Colonel
Comdg. 8 Rl Munster Fusrs

Army Form C. 2118

WAR DIARY or INTELLIGENCE SUMMARY
(Erase heading not required.)

8th Royal Munster Fusiliers

Place	Date	Hour	Summary of Events and Information	Remarks and references to Appendices
DIVL. RESERVE LA CLYTTE (M.6.d)	24/10/16		Training: Bombing, Bayonet fighting, Physical Drill, Rapid adjustment of Box Respirator, Gas Drill. By permission of the Commanding Officer a Battalion Concert was held in the Y.M.C.A. hut, LA CLYTTE at which the G.O.C. 47th Infantry Brigade was present. Thereafter the 16th Divisional Punchment certificate to the following officers & men:- Lieut. Colonel E. MONTEAGLE-BROWNE. D.S.O. Lieut. M.D. CREGAN. Lieut. + Quarter Master J.T. REGAN. 18020 Sgt. J. MURRAY, 3539 Ser. Cpl. T. LAHIFF, 165 Pte. A. CHAMBERLAIN, 4857 Pte. P. KENNEDY, 2736 C.S.M. J. O'NEILL, 1445 Pte. M. HAYES, 1680 Pte. A. BEARDSLEY, 1675, Pte. T. UPTON, 3811 Cpl. T. DUFFY, 1458 Pte. E.P. QUIRKE.	
	25/10/16		Training: Bombing, Bayonet fighting, Physical Drill, Sniping, Machine Gun Section on Range. Capt. 16R & T. WRAFFER S.I. Co. returns from leave.	
	26/10/16		The Battalion fell in at 10 AM. for a Route March, proceeding to SCHERPENBERG via LA CLYTTE, Bn: Sketch order. Order of march: Signallers, Drums, A Coy, M.G. Section, H.C.D. Corps, 3 Coy. Presented to General Instruction at Gas School, CANADA CORNER. The following has been received by G.O.C. 27th Inf. Bde. from Mr. JOHN REDMOND M.P. "Dear General PEREIRA, will you allow me to send you a few lines officially congratulation not only on the magnificent record of the 16th Division but in a special way the	

J Monteagle Browne
Lieut Colonel
Comdg 8th Rl. Muns. Fus.

WAR DIARY or INTELLIGENCE SUMMARY

Army Form C. 2118

8th Royal Munster Fusiliers

Place	Date	Hour	Summary of Events and Information	Remarks and references to Appendices
DIVL RESERVE LA CLYTTE (M.G.d)	26/10/16		record of the 47th Infantry Brigade. We in IRELAND have acted with the greatest pride of this Gallantry & only wish it were in our power still to have the privilege of being associated in the Western front in having so worthily maintained the tradition of our nation.	
"	27/10/16		Training, Bayonet fighting, Bombing + Physical Drill. Machine Gunners and Snipers on range. Also Arms Drill, Close Order Drill and Saluting Drill for Company. By kind permission of the Commanding Officer. A football (Rugby) match was played between composed of officers drawn from this battalion, against A squadron R.F.C. 2 Lieut H.B. Fisher rejoined from hospital this date.	K.C.B
"	28/10/16		Training, Bayonet fighting, Physical Training, Bombing, Close Order, Saluting and Arms Drill, Machine Gunners and Snipers on range. OFFICERS. CAPT J.H. HALL and 2LT POLLOCK reported themselves on 27-10-16. 2LT POLLOCK was admitted to Hospital this day. CAPT. F.S. WOODLEY took over command of 43rd Coy with effect from 27-10-16 *[signature]* 8 R.M. Munster Fusiliers batt.	q.(0)

WAR DIARY or INTELLIGENCE SUMMARY

Army Form C. 2118

Place	Date	Hour	Summary of Events and Information	Remarks and references to Appendices
DIVL RESERVE LA CLYTTE (M.6.d.)	28-10-16 (con)		CAPT J.H. HALL Took over Command of 'C' Coy with effect from 27-10-16. Handing over Certificates duly received. LIEUT D. ARCEDECKNE-BUTLER took over duties of ADJUTANT from 27-10-16 vice LIEUT & ADJT FITZ-GERALD proceeded on leave. 2ND LIEUT HARTIGAN reported his arrival from 2nd Army Sch. of Sniping on 27-10-16. 2 LT R.T. Pollock was admitted to hospital 28-10-16	AA
DE SUPPORT SIEGE FARM (N.16.c.2.1)	29-10-16		SUNDAY DIVINE SERVICE R.C. was held at LA CLYTTE Church at 8.15 a.m. The battalion marched to church with the Pipes & Drums. The battalion relieved a portion of the 7th Leinster Regt at SIEGE FM and KEMMEL. Relief was reported complete at 12.30 pm. After relief dispositions were as follows. Head quarters, C & D Coys at SIEGE FARM (N.16.c.2.1) A & B Coys at KEMMEL. The following appointments (List no 105 of Appointment Commissioned) were noted. Temp. Lieut F.S. WOODLEY to be acting Captain whilst commanding a Coy. 5-10-16. Temp Lieut F.J. BIGGANE to be transferred to General List for duty with 49th	AB

J.B.C. &A. A.D.S.S./Forms/C. 2118.

WAR DIARY
or
INTELLIGENCE SUMMARY

Army Form C. 2118

Place	Date	Hour	Summary of Events and Information	Remarks and references to Appendices
BDE SUPPORT SIEGE FARM (N.16.C.27)	29-10-16		2Lt F.J. PARROTT rejoined off leave this date.	
"	30-10-16		Training. Coys were at the disposal of Coy Officers for dealing with Box respirators &c. Working Parties supplied according to programme. The undermentioned played at football:- 2Lt J.P. McCRUBEN reported his arrival from 2nd Army Sch. of Bombing. Pte. G. DONNELLY reported his arrival from 3rd Army Sch. of Musketry.	A.C.I.D
"	31-10-16		The usual Working parties were supplied. The M.O. held a conference with all Coy. Officers. O.C. Coys also instructed to give lecturers on Sniping, Mills on Physical training etc. All Ranks were recommended. The Band played at retreat. 2Lt E.P. HARTIGAN is appointed Sniping Officer. 2Lt J.F. FULLIN admitted to hospital. No other ranks reported arrival.	A.6.D

E Montague Lt Col O.C.

Cmds 6th Rl. Innis. Fus. S. Colonel

WAR DIARY.

FOR

MONTH OF NOVEMBER, 1916.

VOLUME 12.

8th R. Munster Fusiliers

Army Form C. 2118.

WAR DIARY
or
INTELLIGENCE SUMMARY.
(Erase heading not required.)

Instructions regarding War Diaries and Intelligence Summaries are contained in F. S. Regs., Part II. and the Staff Manual respectively. Title pages will be prepared in manuscript.

Place	Date	Hour	Summary of Events and Information	Remarks and references to Appendices
SUPPORT				
BATTN				
SIEGE				
FARM				
(N 40 c 2)				
LEFT				
SECTOR				
10th DIVISIONAL				
AREA				

T2134. Wt. W708—776. 500000. 4/15. Sir J. C. & S.

Army Form C. 2118.

WAR DIARY
or
INTELLIGENCE SUMMARY.
(Erase heading not required.)

Instructions regarding War Diaries and Intelligence Summaries are contained in F. S. Regs., Part II. and the Staff Manual respectively. Title pages will be prepared in manuscript.

Place	Date	Hour	Summary of Events and Information	Remarks and references to Appendices
LEFT SECTOR XI DIVISIONAL AREA	4.11.16		LT MANNIP offered to L Col y CAPTAIN SCHOOL on command of Company. Bn. ARTILLERY forwarded the enquiry for 75mm shells of type after his hr.p. Lived on terms the front line. 238 OR LEAVE. Received LT I. REID who for present 230 H.Qs steady. RMM his Co.	
	5.11.16		PTE J. NONAN of B Coy from wounds received by [illegible] 2 LT KIM 7th PLOT stretcher bearer party. 2/30 TRIMBLE to A Raid over the top I.O. letter on the enemy front line by 2 Lt Lumsden. Proceeded the enemy trench on the Battle Gustra in front. The party were covered by Lewis gun fire from [illegible] trenches & assisted myself by grenadiers [illegible] not been met with & return [illegible]	

Wm W Elliott Lt Col SRA F

Army Form C. 2118.

WAR DIARY
or
INTELLIGENCE SUMMARY.
(Erase heading not required.)

Instructions regarding War Diaries and Intelligence Summaries are contained in F. S. Regs., Part II. and the Staff Manual respectively. Title pages will be prepared in manuscript.

Place	Date	Hour	Summary of Events and Information	Remarks and references to Appendices
BDE Reserve BUTTERFLY FARM (M19A6.4)		1–4pm	A report received that Lt M.... Capt T.F. Skelton 2Lt F. Morrow [...] Capt T.H. Hall wounded at Bn ... M.M., Lt ... R.......	

Army Form C. 2118.

WAR DIARY
or
INTELLIGENCE SUMMARY.
(Erase heading not required.)

Instructions regarding War Diaries and Intelligence Summaries are contained in F. S. Regs., Part II. and the Staff Manual respectively. Title pages will be prepared in manuscript.

Place	Date	Hour	Summary of Events and Information	Remarks and references to Appendices

Army Form C. 2118.

WAR DIARY
or
INTELLIGENCE SUMMARY.
(Erase heading not required.)

Instructions regarding War Diaries and Intelligence Summaries are contained in F. S. Regs., Part II. and the Staff Manual respectively. Title pages will be prepared in manuscript.

Place	Date	Hour	Summary of Events and Information	Remarks and references to Appendices

T2134. Wt. W708—776. 500000. 4/15. Sir J. C. & S.

Army Form C. 2118.

WAR DIARY
or
INTELLIGENCE SUMMARY.
(Erase heading not required.)

Instructions regarding War Diaries and Intelligence Summaries are contained in F. S. Regs., Part II. and the Staff Manual respectively. Title pages will be prepared in manuscript.

Place	Date	Hour	Summary of Events and Information	Remarks and references to Appendices

T2134. Wt. W708—776. 500000. 4/15. Sir J. C. & S.

Army Form C. 2118.

WAR DIARY
or
INTELLIGENCE SUMMARY.
(Erase heading not required.)

Instructions regarding War Diaries and Intelligence Summaries are contained in F. S. Regs., Part II. and the Staff Manual respectively. Title pages will be prepared in manuscript.

Place	Date	Hour	Summary of Events and Information	Remarks and references to Appendices

T.J.34. Wt. W708—776. 500000. 4/15. Sir J. C. & S.

Army Form C. 2118.

WAR DIARY
or
INTELLIGENCE SUMMARY.
(Erase heading not required.)

Instructions regarding War Diaries and Intelligence Summaries are contained in F.S. Regs., Part II. and the Staff Manual respectively. Title pages will be prepared in manuscript.

Place	Date	Hour	Summary of Events and Information	Remarks and references to Appendices

Army Form C. 2118.

WAR DIARY
or
INTELLIGENCE SUMMARY.
(Erase heading not required.)

Instructions regarding War Diaries and Intelligence Summaries are contained in F. S. Regs., Part II. and the Staff Manual respectively. Title pages will be prepared in manuscript.

Place	Date	Hour	Summary of Events and Information	Remarks and references to Appendices

T2134. Wt. W708—776. 500000. 4/15. Sir J. C. & S.

Army Form C. 2118.

WAR DIARY
or
INTELLIGENCE SUMMARY.
(Erase heading not required.)

Instructions regarding War Diaries and Intelligence Summaries are contained in F. S. Regs., Part II. and the Staff Manual respectively. Title pages will be prepared in manuscript.

Place	Date	Hour	Summary of Events and Information	Remarks and references to Appendices

www.ingramcontent.com/pod-product-compliance
Lightning Source LLC
Chambersburg PA
CBHW081426160426

43193CB00013B/2204